# CONTENTS

# INTRODUCTION: A TRIP BACK IN TIME

The truth is, we don't know much about the early history of the human race.

Most of what we do know goes back only five thousand years, to the time when written language was first invented. Before that time, we only have whatever was handed down by word of mouth.

As far back as the cavemen, the elders of tribes would gather around the fire to tell younger members stories of the olden days. Sometimes, these stories would be in the form of long poems called epics, about heroic events and leaders. Other times, they would be myths or legends, explaining some of the many mysteries of nature.

On the walls of certain caves, you can still see ancient drawings of hunts and campfires, surrounded by the handprints of the artists. Were they illustrations for the stories the elders told?

When we hear such myths or legends today, it's important to realize that while some events might really have happened, they probably didn't happen exactly as the story tells it. But that doesn't make the stories less beautiful, or less meaningful. They can still have important lessons to teach us, and are fascinating, besides.

This is a story about events that took place in ancient India, before writing reached that part of the world—a story that has come down to us by word of mouth, about an amazing man and the wonderful gift of wisdom he left us all.

Did the Buddha really exist? Probably. Did everything in his life story really happen? Maybe—but like any story, the Buddha's has changed over the centuries, growing larger than life.

One thing is certain: The teachings of the Buddha have been a great help to billions of people, for thousands of years. And as he himself said before he died, "Look for me in my teaching."

So we will. But first, we've got to take a trip back in time—to the world of ancient northern India, where the child who would become *the Buddha* was born. . . .

Around the time humans learned to write, the ancient wonders of the world were being built—the great pyramids of Egypt, the Hanging Gardens of Babylon, the Colossus of Rhodes. Each of the civilizations that built them had its own unique religion. For instance, the people of ancient India worshipped the Earth Goddess, also called the Great Mother.

Around 1500 B.C., invaders from Central Asia called Aryans conquered the peaceful civilizations of northern India. The Aryans brought their own religion with them. They replaced Earth Goddess worship with their own belief in many gods, the greatest of whom was Indra. In the Aryans' religion, the gods did not live forever. Far from perfect, they lived, died, and behaved pretty much like ordinary people.

The priests of this Aryan religion were called Brahmins. The Brahmins became the leading class, or "caste," of Aryan society. Ruling along with them were the Kshatriyas—princes, kings, and warriors. Below these two castes were the Vaisyas, or merchants, and the Sudras, who were little better than slaves.

Each of these four castes was divided into many subcastes. Each subcaste performed only a certain set of jobs, and no others. Vaisyas could not be priests. Kshatriyas could not collect garbage—that job was too low even for Sudras!

For such work, there were classes below the Sudras. These were the Panchamas, or outcasts (outcastes). Because it was forbidden even to touch these people, they became known as "untouchables." (This system still exists in India today, although laws forbid discrimination based on caste. Old customs, it seems, are very hard to change.)

The Aryans' religion, Brahmanism, was so complicated that only Brahmins could understand it. They held ceremonies in their own language (Sanskrit). Most local people could not understand a word they said! There were many ceremonies and rituals, but people found them boring and only joined in because they were afraid the gods would be angry if they didn't.

Brahmanism taught that when people die, they are reincarnated—that is, reborn—over and over again. If you were good in this life, you would have a better life next time. If you were bad, you would come back to a worse existence—as a bug, or perhaps as a snake. So it was important to be good, and to suffer quietly, since innocent suffering in this life would lead to greater happiness in the next.

Most people were unsatisfied with their fate. They longed for a religious leader who could offer them some hope of contentment in *this* life!

★ ★ ★ ★

By the year 563 B.C., the Aryan civilizations of northern India had crumbled, replaced by dozens of small, warring kingdoms. People flocked to cities for protection, work, and the chance to make money.

Still, most people lived in poverty and misery. Their religion told them they were doomed to suffer forever, in life after life, until they finally reached *Nirvana*—enlightenment—and were liberated from the endless cycle of death and rebirth.

A few small kingdoms and republics, most in out-of-the-way places, managed to steer clear of trouble, and to stay peaceful and independent. These places did not follow the caste system as rigidly as everywhere else.

One of these small states was called Sakya. No one would remember it today, except for one thing: Sakya was the birthplace of Prince Siddhartha Gautama, who would change the world forever, and who became known as "the Enlightened One"—*the Buddha*.

# CHAPTER ONE

# A MIRACULOUS BIRTH

The little kingdom of Sakya lay in the far north of India, near the great mountains of the Himalaya range. In fact, if you looked up from Lord Shuddhodana Gautama's great walled castle, over the treetops of the forests that surrounded his capital city, Kapilavastu, you could see their snowcapped peaks.

It was a beautiful land, and Shuddhodana ruled it well. He was not a king exactly. Sakya was a republic, ruled by the warrior class, Kshatriyas, of whom he was the highest ranking.

His first wife, Maya (men were allowed more than one in those days), and second wife, Japiti, were sisters. Both women were daughters of the king of Koliya, to the east of Sakya. Because of this, Koliya was a friendly neighbor. Such could not be said of the kingdoms to the south, however. Lord Shuddhodana worried that one day they would attack Sakya, conquer it, and enslave his people.

How he longed for a son, one who would grow to be a strong leader and keep Sakya free—perhaps even make it larger and greater! Shuddhodana and Maya had prayed for a child for twenty long years, but their prayers had gone unanswered.

Then one morning, Maya woke her husband and said, "I had a strange and wonderful dream last night. A great white elephant with six tusks came to me on a mountaintop and pierced my side with its trunk. I felt a warm, golden feeling, and my heart was filled with gladness."

The lord summoned his wise men—all Brahmins—and asked them the meaning of Maya's dream. (People in those days believed that certain dreams were messages from the gods.)

"The queen will have a child," said the Brahmins. "And what a child! It shall be a boy—a holy child of amazing wisdom, who will grow up to benefit the whole world."

"Ah! A great ruler—just what I have been praying for!" shouted Shuddhodana happily.

"He will rule, if he chooses to rule," said the eldest Brahmin.

"What do you mean *if*?" asked Shuddhodana.

"He may turn out to be a great king or conqueror, or he may become a great sage. It is entirely up to him."

"We'll see about that," said Shuddhodana, frowning. "I am his father, after all."

He dismissed the Brahmins. Then he breathed deeply, turned to Maya, and smiled. "This little boy of ours will lead Sakya to glory," he said. "I will see to it that he makes the correct choice."

Outside the lord's chamber, the youngest of the Brahmins, Kondanna, turned to his elder colleague. "Why did you tell the lord that his son might be either a king or a sage?"

"Because that is the meaning of Lady Maya's dream," said the elder Brahmin.

"That is not what I saw," said Kondanna. "There is only one path for this child."

The older Brahmin put a hand on Kondanna's shoulder. "I am glad you did not mention it to Lord Shuddhodana. He has enough troubles on his mind."

"But—"

"Whatever is to be, shall be. It does no good to speak the truth when it cannot help."

In those days, it was the custom for women who were about to give birth to visit their parents' home and have the baby there. So Maya and her sister Japiti, who was also going to have a child, decided to make the trip to their father's palace.

They were accompanied by many servants and friends, and they began their journey in fine weather. It was late in the month of May. The sun shone brightly during the day, and the moon was nearly full at night.

They had not gone very far when Maya realized that she was about to have her baby. The traveling party stopped at Lumbini Park, a grove of straight, tall trees. There, the servants prepared a soft bed of flowers for Maya beneath a great sandalwood tree. Legend says that the tree kindly bent down one of its branches so that Lady Maya could hang on to it for support while she gave birth.

Like Jesus more than five hundred years later, the Buddha-to-be was born in simple surroundings, during a halt on a journey.

All of nature rejoiced at his birth, the legend continues. Rainbows appeared everywhere in the sky, bitter enemies hugged one another, and a great feeling of happiness, love, and peace covered the land.

Even in the great Himalaya Mountains to the north, there were omens. There, wise men called *yogis* who lived in caves, far from people, cities, and the noise of civilization, noticed the joyful signs nature was displaying. They realized that something wonderful must have happened.

The greatest sage of them all, Asita, went into a deep meditation—a visionary trance—and saw that a very special child had been born. He made his way to Kapilavastu at once—and arrived so soon after the birth of the prince that people said he must have flown through the air, or else transported himself there by a miracle.

Now that the baby had been born, the traveling party turned around and headed home to Kapilavastu. On their way they passed the farms, forests, towns, and villages of Sakya. Everywhere, people gathered to see the newborn child. Many followed the procession back to the capital, where Lord Shuddhodana waited impatiently to see his son for the first time, and people were streaming into the city from far and wide to admire the new prince.

During the celebrations, the yogi Asita asked permission to see the baby, whom his parents named Siddhartha—"he who has achieved his goal." Shuddhodana and Maya were honored that the great sage had come all the way from the Himalayas to see their son.

Asita examined the baby for signs of holiness, visible only to a great sage like him. He found many such signs on Siddhartha—such as a golden light shining from the baby's fingertips. There were thirty-two signs in all, and Siddhartha had every one of them!

Afterward, when Shuddhodana and Maya laid the baby at Asita's feet for a blessing, the sage shook his head and said, "No, it is I who must bow down before him."

Shuddhodana said, "Great sage, my wise men have told me that the boy will be the most powerful ruler in the world someday. Is that what you mean?"

"He will become the greatest being in the world," said Asita, weeping.

"Why do you weep?" asked Maya. "Is something wrong?"

"No. I weep only because I will not live to see it," said Asita, who was already very old. "I will not be able to hear his teachings in this life."

"His teachings? What do you mean?"

"It is in his teachings that his power will lie."

"I do not understand," said Shuddhodana. "Will he not be a king, Asita?"

"He will be something even greater."

"Even greater? What are you talking about?" asked Shuddhodana. "You don't mean that he'll be a monk like you, living in some cave high on a mountain, or wandering the roads and forests with a beggar's bowl in his hands?"

"Rejoice, my Lord," Asita replied, "for your son will attain true enlightenment. When he sees how all the world suffers, it will affect him deeply, and set him on his path."

"His path? What path do you mean?"

Asita wiped the tears from his cheeks. "His path is the road to Nirvana. More than that, I cannot say."

As he watched the great sage depart, Shuddhodana was troubled about the sage's prediction for his son's future. Siddhartha was clearly going to be a very special person—but what kind?

Shuddhodana was determined that the boy grow up to rule the world as a good and strong king. The other choice, becoming a sage, did not please him. One could only become a sage by spending years as a poor wandering *ascetic*.

These ascetics were well respected for their devotion, but by tradition, they had to live out in the open and beg for their food. They ate only one simple meal a day, had no money, no wives or children—nothing at all, in fact!

The very thought of Siddhartha choosing that life over the glorious life of a king worried Shuddhodana tremendously. He respected ascetics, yogis, and all sorts of holy men, but that was something for a person to do when he had finished his work in this world!

Perhaps when he was old, Siddhartha could set aside his kingly crown to seek holiness. But only *after* he had become the greatest king on Earth. . . .

The next day, Shuddhodana sent for his

Brahmins. "You all heard what the sage Asita said. My son will cast away his kingdom and become a beggar! Tell me, is there no way to stop this from happening?"

The Brahmins cast frightened glances at one another. Finally, the eldest one spoke. "Your Lordship, there is a way to insure that your son will be the great king you hope for, and bring honor to your line and to Sakya."

"What is that way? I must know!" Shuddhodana said excitedly.

"Prince Siddhartha is very sensitive," said the old Brahmin. "He must never see how the world suffers outside these castle walls. If he sees old age, sickness, death—if he sees that there are people in this world, ascetic yogis who give up everything and even starve themselves almost to death in search of holiness—if he sees all these things, there is no hope."

"In that case," the lord said, "he must never see them. I will make sure he knows nothing of evil, or sadness. His life will be filled with beauty and riches, music, dance, and all the pleasures of this world. Thus will he become the great king that he is meant to be."

# CHAPTER TWO

# A GOLDEN CHILDHOOD

Soon after the days of celebration ended, Lord Shuddhodana's attention turned to a new crisis. Lady Maya, the new mother, suddenly grew sick and feverish. None of the palace's healers or wise men could help her, and her condition got worse and worse. Soon it was clear to one and all that she was dying.

Just before the end, Maya called her sister and fellow queen to her bedside. Japiti herself was due to give birth any day. "I beg you, Japiti," Maya whispered, "take care of my son Siddhartha. Nurse him as you do your own child. Be a mother to him when I am gone. Promise me you will do this."

"I will, sister," said Japiti.

Maya had the promise she wanted. She closed her eyes for the last time, and soon passed from this world.

The next day, Japiti gave birth. Keeping her promise, she nursed little Siddhartha, giving her own baby to a wet nurse to feed.

Lord Shuddhodana could not contain his grief over the loss of his favorite wife. But the baby Siddhartha, only seven days old, seemed happy and content. He quickly accepted Japiti as his mother.

As for Japiti, she loved Siddhartha as if he were her own son. And after all, it was not a hard job to love and care for such a golden child. He was handsome and well formed, with wonderful, penetrating eyes and a smile that made you feel warm all over.

He was soon walking, then running and climbing like a child twice his age. He was wonderfully good-tempered, and almost never cried. He was polite and obedient to his elders, gentle with his servants, and kind to everyone he met.

Siddhartha's life was filled with beauty, riches, and pleasure, just as his father had planned it. He wore the finest silks, and woven cloth from the great city of Benares. Always, a servant held an umbrella over his head so the hot sun would not bother him. He ate the tastiest, rarest foods and knew only young, healthy people—for anyone old or sick was kept far from his sight.

He spent all his days within the beautiful walled gardens of the palace grounds. His playmates were the children of other nobles, many of them his cousins. Siddhartha was smarter, taller, and more athletic than any of them, and had the nicest personality besides. He loved everyone, and everyone loved him back.

Well, *almost* everyone. His cousin Devadatta was more than a little jealous. If not for Siddhartha, *he* would have been the tallest, the handsomest, the best at everything from archery to wrestling. (But more about Devadatta later . . .)

Siddhartha was a quiet boy, though when he

did speak, he always said something worth hearing. Although he was the best athlete among his playmates, he didn't play at sports with them very often. He liked wrestling and archery well enough, but he beat all the other boys so easily that after a while, it wasn't much fun anymore.

He preferred to sit in the palace gardens, watching the birds, insects, and other small animals as they went about their business. *How beautiful they are,* he thought happily. *How perfect.* Looking around, it seemed to him that everything was beautiful and perfect. Everyone was happy. The whole world was at peace.

Of course, he did not know what life was like beyond the castle gate, out in the streets of the capital city and beyond, on the farms and in the forests, even in the mountains. He was a young child, who had never been outside these walls. In his innocence, he imagined that things must be just as wonderful everywhere else.

Lord Shuddhodana stood at the window of

his chamber, high above the gardens, and watched his son sitting on the ground by the lotus pool. *What is he looking at?* he wondered to himself. *A butterfly?*

He smiled at the sight of his little boy, so happy, so content. Shuddhodana intended to keep him that way for as long as possible.

The sage Asita had said his son would be deeply affected by the sight of suffering. Very well, then—Siddhartha would not see any suffering. *Ever.* "Well, at least not until he is much older and more mature," Shuddhodana muttered. "If then."

When he was seven years old, Shuddhodana decided that Siddhartha should finally be allowed to leave the palace grounds. If he was going to be a great ruler someday, sooner or later he had to start learning the duties of a future king.

One of these duties was to attend the annual Planting Festival. Each year at the beginning of spring plowing, Sakyans celebrated. Before they could till their land and plant their crops, the gods had to be honored. So their high lord, Shuddhodana, himself drove the first plow over the ground. That year, Shuddhodana decided to bring Siddhartha with him.

Outside the castle walls for the first time in his life, Siddhartha marveled at the wonders of Kapilavastu, the capital city. So many palaces and mansions, markets and homes! And all so bright and cheerful . . . Everyone was dressed in colorful holiday clothing.

On Lord Shuddhodana's orders, the city had been cleared of anyone whose appearance might disturb the prince. The old, the ugly, the disabled, and the sick were forbidden to show their faces. No funerals were permitted, and no burning of the dead, as was commonly done throughout the lands of India.

Siddhartha stood beside his father as he drove a pair of bullocks, who wore silver harnesses and pulled a silver plow. The people cheered as the plow cut into the rich brown earth, turning it over so that it was ready for planting.

But what was this? Those worms had been cut in two by the sharp blades of the plow! Siddhartha watched as the two halves of the worm twisted in pain. Then a small bird swooped down and ate first one of the halves, then the other.

No sooner had the bird finished the second worm than a nearby hawk swooped down and caught the little bird in its claws, killing it. The big bird flew off with its meal, and Siddhartha watched with tears in his eyes.

Finally, Shuddhodana noticed that his son was no longer enjoying the festival. "What is it?" he asked the boy.

Siddhartha could not answer. He was so upset, he could not even speak.

"Take him to rest for a while," Shuddhodana told the servants.

Siddhartha was led to a soft, silk-covered couch under a spreading rose-apple tree. There, they left him to rest.

Alone with his thoughts, Siddhartha closed his eyes and breathed deeply, trying to forget what he had just seen, to let go of the horrible images of death and pain. He paid attention only to his breathing, and so deeply did he meditate that he soon fell into a trance—the first mystical experience of his life.

The attendants found him there when they returned. So deep was the boy's trance, they reported, that the shadow of the rose-apple tree did not move for hours. Perhaps they were exaggerating, but there is no doubt that they were impressed with the depth of the boy's concentration, and the power of his being.

When Siddhartha was eight years old, Lord Shuddhodana decided it was time to begin the prince's education. So he arranged for the best tutor he could find. But after only a few days, the teacher asked to see him.

"I cannot teach this child," he told the lord.

"But why?" asked Shuddhodana, frowning. "Has he been behaving badly?"

"No, no! He is always well mannered and polite, and does everything I ask of him."

"Then what is the problem?" asked Shuddhodana.

"He already knows everything I have to teach him!" exclaimed the teacher. "Well, *almost* everything. He must have had another teacher before me."

"No—you are the first, I assure you."

"Incredible. Simply incredible . . . the boy is a genius! He has already learned languages, and mathematics . . . and . . . and . . . he's even taught me a thing or two!"

Lord Shuddhodana hired other teachers, but the same thing happened over and over again. Finally, Shuddhodana decided that they would all supervise Siddhartha's lessons together—even if the boy knew more than any of them.

There was nothing else to be done. Siddhartha had to be kept within the walls of the palace. Otherwise, there was no telling what might happen.

★　★　★　★

Shuddhodana ordered three new palaces to be built for his son, one for each season of the year: winter, summer, and rainy season. By the time he was grown up, they would be finished, and Lord Siddhartha would have his choice of splendid places to live. With three palaces to choose from, Siddhartha would always be comfortable.

The best part was that all three palaces were built inside a huge area of parkland and forest. Siddhartha could wander in nature to his heart's content, watching the animals and plants he loved so well, all within three sets of thick, high walls that would keep the world and its suffering far from his eyes and ears.

Siddhartha indeed loved to be out in nature. He was strolling the grounds of his father's palace with his cousin Devadatta one spring day, just the two of them. Lately, Siddhartha had noticed that Devadatta seemed unhappy, so he'd invited him for the day, and Devadatta was happy to accept. This sign of affection from his cousin made him feel special for once.

Devadatta had brought along his new bow and arrows—"to practice my archery," he told Siddhartha. The two boys had often shot at targets together, but Siddhartha had given it up after a while, because Devadatta always got so upset when Siddhartha did better, and he'd gotten tired of letting Devadatta win.

Devadatta mistakenly thought Siddhartha had given up because he couldn't keep up as Devadatta improved. Now, he was determined to show his cousin how well he could shoot— by hitting a moving target.

For his part, Siddhartha knew nothing of his cousin's plan. After a while, he tired of walking and sat down on a flat rock to watch a pair of sparrows build their nest.

Devadatta wandered ahead some distance on his own, and Siddhartha forgot about him as the busy birds wove a nest of grass and twigs.

*Nature is so wonderful,* he thought, looking up at the sky as a pair of swans flew by.

THWACK!

An arrow flew through the air and struck one of the swans in the wing. The other flew off in terror as the wounded bird fluttered and fell to the ground.

Siddhartha was shocked and upset. He ran straight to where the bird had fallen and saw that it was in pain. Taking it firmly in his arms, he removed the arrow. "It's all right," he cooed gently in the bird's ear, "I won't hurt you."

Then he reached over to grab some buds from a nearby pagoda tree. From his lessons he had learned that these buds could stop bleeding and help heal wounds.

He crushed the buds in his fingers, and the juice ran onto the swan's wing. Quickly, it stopped bleeding.

"Don't worry, dear bird," Siddhartha cooed into the swan's ear, calming it. "I'll take care of you until the wound heals and you're well enough to fly. Then you can go find your mate."

He removed his fine silk shirt and wrapped

the swan in it. "There," he said. "A nice, soft, warm bed for you."

"HEY!"

Devadatta appeared from behind some trees. "That swan's mine! I shot it."

"I saved its life," Siddhartha replied. "It belongs to me."

"Give it to me!" Devadatta demanded.

"I won't."

Devadatta balled his hands into fists. "I shot that bird on my very first try—it's my very first kill!"

"It's not dead."

For a moment, Devadatta thought of trying to grab the bird from his cousin's grasp. But he knew Siddhartha was stronger than he was. "All right, then," he said, picking up his arrow. "But that bird is mine. You took it—and I'm telling."

"Fine," said Siddhartha. "Better yet—why don't we let the Brahmins decide?"

The king's wise men were summoned to the grove, and agreed to decide which was right.

Both boys argued their cases well, and the Brahmins were undecided, until an old, wandering monk appeared.

"I was just strolling down the path," he told the Brahmins, "and I happened to overhear the arguments." He cleared his throat and gave a little bow of the head. "Might I . . . offer a humble opinion?"

The Brahmins looked at one another. "Why not?" they decided. "He is a holy man. Let us hear what he has to say."

The old man bowed again, then said: "If life is worth anything at all—if it is just the least bit precious—then he who saves it is surely more worthy than he who takes it."

"He is right!" said the Brahmins. "The old monk has spoken the truth—Siddhartha must have the swan!"

They turned to thank the wandering monk for his wise council, but the old man was gone—just as though he had vanished into thin air.

"It must have been a *god*!" said the eldest

Brahmin, and the others nodded in agreement.

If, once again, the child Siddhartha had proven to be a favorite of the gods, why should any of them have been surprised? From the moment of his birth, and even before, the heavenly signs had all pointed to a great destiny for him.

Siddhartha sat there, stroking his swan, while Devadatta stormed off angrily.

"This is not the end," he muttered to himself, clenching his fists. "It is only the beginning. You wait and see, Siddhartha—you haven't heard the last of Devadatta yet!"

# CHAPTER THREE
# YASODHARA

Siddhartha sat on the silk cushions of the stone bench by the lotus pond. A baby antelope, drinking with its mother, saw him and wandered over to his side.

From his bedroom in the palace, Shuddhodana also watched his sixteen-year-old son. "It is amazing the way wild animals come right up to him, unafraid."

"His nature is golden," Japiti said, watching beside him. "Holy, even."

Shuddhodana drew away from her, frowning. "Holy? Do not call him that—ever again! He must not think of holiness—not until he has become a great king and ensured the succession of the Gautama line by having sons of his own."

"What is it that troubles you so, my love?" Japiti asked.

"He is so . . . so moody," said Shuddhodana, still staring down at his son.

The antelope faun had returned to its mother's side. Siddhartha was dipping his toes into the water of the lotus pond, staring at the circular ripples on the water's surface. "Much too dreamy, if you ask me."

"Do not worry so much," Japiti said. "He is the strongest and fastest of all the boys at the palace—and also quite good with the bow and arrow."

"Yes, but he won't kill anything! What sort of an archer is that?"

"A kind and gentle one," she replied, putting a soothing hand on his shoulder. "One who will lead well, and will always be beloved by all the world."

"Perhaps," Shuddhodana said, but he was not convinced.

He looked at his son sitting there, staring at the water for what seemed like hours! It was like he was in a trance—oh, yes, he often did that. And none of his teachers could explain it, other than to say he would make a wonderful holy man.

*Holy—that word again!*

Lord Shuddhodana summoned his Brahmins that very afternoon. "My son is growing to manhood," he told them, "yet he is still like a child. He dreams his days away in the garden, and seems to be in another world!"

The Brahmins consulted with one another, and then the eldest spoke. "Lord Shuddhodana," he said, "the young prince dreams of other worlds because he has no life in this one."

"No life?"

"What are his responsibilities? He may not leave the palace grounds, he is always surrounded by teachers who don't know as much as he does, and by servants who never let him do anything for himself. So he yearns to escape, to be alone, to dream of other worlds."

"Well, what is the solution?" Shuddhodana asked.

The Brahmins all smiled and looked at the eldest, who answered, "My Lord, you must find the prince a bride!"

"A bride? But he is only . . . how old is he?"

"Sixteen, My Lord."

"Sixteen already? Hmm . . . perhaps you are right."

"Indeed, My Lord. Once he finds himself attached to someone he loves, with children to care about, he will stop this dreaming of other worlds. His life in *this* world will be rich and satisfying. Then, and only then, will he be interested in becoming a great king."

Shuddhodana smiled. "Thank you, my wise men. You are wise indeed. It shall be as you say."

Before there could be a wedding, there had to be a bride. And not just any bride, but one worthy of such a golden prince! Shuddhodana sent his messengers to all the neighboring kingdoms and republics, announcing that Prince Siddhartha meant to choose a princess.

"Any lord who thinks his daughter worthy, let him send her to Kapilavastu," the messengers cried, in every public square of every capital city in the region. "Three months from now, on the night of the full moon, there will be a great banquet at Lord Shuddhodana's palace. And on that very night, Prince Siddhartha will choose his bride!"

Preparations for the grand feast began. At the palace in Kapilavastu, there were constant comings and goings. The great room of the palace was big enough for five hundred guests, but there would easily be that many present— for each young lady had to be accompanied by her family or chaperone, and by her servants, of course.

In many neighboring lands, silk merchants were busy making the dresses, called saris, that the young women would need to impress the prince. Jewelers, goldsmiths, and silversmiths did a brisk business adorning the would-be brides.

Finally, the great day came. Prince Siddhartha

was dressed by servants in the finest silk and jewels. He allowed everything to happen around him—but inside, he remained dreamy, bored with all the fuss.

Ever since that first Planting Festival he'd attended at the age of seven, he'd had the feeling there was much, much more to the world than he knew. His life was pleasant enough, yet he was guarded like a prisoner—by order of Lord Shuddhodana himself.

*Well, let my father have it his way,* thought Siddhartha. *Until now, I have been his loyal child. But once I am married, I will no longer be a child. Even he must see that it is so, and allow me to go out on my own, unattended and free.*

All the guests had now arrived, and the maidens with their attendants filed into the great hall. Everyone *oohed* and *aahed* at the great beauty and finery on display. Surely the prince would find a wonderful bride tonight!

Finally, it was time for Siddhartha's grand entrance. Everyone stood and gazed at him as he walked in—so handsome was he, so tall and pleasing to look at. He gazed around the room at all the young women who had come with hopes of being his wife. As he glanced at each of them in turn, they blushed and looked away, smiling with pleasure. Only one held his gaze—he tried to get a better look at her, but she was soon lost in the crowd.

Siddhartha took his seat, and the banquet began. Talented musicians from as far away as Persia played beautiful tunes as the guests feasted on the finest foods and drink.

After the plates were cleared away, the servants brought a large golden tray filled with precious jewels, all in little silk boxes. They placed the tray in front of Siddhartha. It was time for the evening's business to begin.

One by one, each girl came up to the table and presented herself to the prince with a little bow. He returned the courtesy, placing his palms together in front of his face and nodding, saying, *"Namaste."* ("I salute the higher nature in you.") Then he took a gift from the tray and gave one to each girl, looking her in the eyes.

All the young ladies looked away, unable to hold the prince's intense gaze. Each one returned to her seat, clutching her gift, and quickly ripped open the box to see what it contained. Gasps of pleasure followed as they beheld the precious jewels inside.

As the girls took turns, one after the other, Lord Shuddhodana leaned over to Lady Japiti and whispered, "See how bored and uninterested he looks?"

"Indeed he does," she agreed. "I do not think he likes any of them, as beautiful as they are."

"If he does not see fit to marry *any* of them, I do not know what I will do next," Lord Shuddhodana confided.

"It will do no good to force the prince to marry someone whom he does not love," Japiti said. "That will not make him happier, or more interested in being a king."

As the last girl came up to face him, everyone suddenly came to attention. Although she was beautiful, she was no more so than the others—yet something was different about this girl. It was the way she walked: gracefully yet so purposefully, too!

As she approached him, Siddhartha recognized her as the one who had not looked down when he entered the hall. "What is your name?" he asked, gazing into her eyes.

Looking right back at him, she replied, "I am Yasodhara, My Lord."

They stood gazing into each other's eyes for a long moment. The entire hall was silent as the guests became aware that something unusual was happening.

"I am so sorry," said Siddhartha, looking down at the empty golden tray, "but I seem to have run out of gifts."

"Do not trouble yourself, My Lord," said Yasodhara. "I did not come here to receive such a gift."

"No?"

"I came in hope of receiving a much greater prize."

Her words went straight to his heart.

Siddhartha removed the ring from his finger and placed it on hers. "Take this ring as your prize, Yasodhara."

A great cheer went up from the guests as everyone understood that Prince Siddhartha had found himself a bride. The other girls consoled themselves with the expensive presents they had received. Still, they were disappointed not to have been chosen, for the prince was such a handsome young man, with such kind eyes.

"Who is the young lady?" Lord Shuddhodana asked his advisers. "She has unsurpassed beauty and grace, I must say. But is she wellborn?"

"She is the Princess Yasodhara," they told him. "Daughter of your neighbor, King Suprabuddha."

"Ah!" said Shuddhodana. "A fine match indeed! The king is a distant cousin of mine, and with this marriage, our families and our nations will be tied more strongly."

He sent for his scribe to come at once. "You

must write a letter to the good king at once, asking for her hand in marriage on Siddhartha's behalf," he told the scribe. "Bring it to me when it is ready so that I may sign it and seal it."

The message was sent, and not many days later the answer came back—but it was not the answer Lord Shuddhodana had been hoping for.

# CHAPTER FOUR

# THE GREAT CONTEST

*My dear cousin, I have read with great joy your letter regarding the marriage of my daughter, the princess, to your son, Siddhartha. I have heard wonderful things about the young prince, and I am honored by your request.*

*But I must tell you honestly, the Princess Yasodhara has many suitors. They have all given precious gifts in hopes of winning her hand. Still, the most important thing is not who gives the richest present, but who is most manly.*

*I have heard great things about young Siddhartha—that he is handsome, gracious, noble, and kind. But I have also heard of his dreaminess and gentleness. I am not sure he will prove to be more manly than his rivals.*

*Among these noble Aryan princes is Devadatta, whom everyone says is a champion with the bow and arrow. Arjuna, the renowned horseman, is another, and so is Nanda, the great swordsman. If your son wishes to wed my daughter, let him meet these young worthies in a contest of skill. He who wins shall have my daughter in marriage.*

*Yours in peace and friendship,*
*Suprabuddha*

Lord Shuddhodana frowned deeply when he read this letter. "I do not like this," he said. "I do not like it at all."

Siddhartha had come into the chamber and he saw what was going on. "Let me see the letter, Father," he said. When he had read it, he smiled. "Do not worry, Father. Let the contest be held. I shall show you—and everyone else—that I am no stranger to the manly arts. I can shoot an arrow, ride a horse, and wield a sword with any man."

Shuddhodana had his doubts, but he ordered the tournament to be held.

The news spread like wildfire that the four young princes—Devadatta, Arjuna, Nanda, and Siddhartha—would compete for Princess Yasodhara's hand. Everyone had heard of her beauty and grace, and they all wondered which prince would prove most worthy of her.

The other contestants were happy to have the chance to show their skills. Each was confident he could best his rivals in his specialty, but worried that he might not win the other two events.

None of them was worried about Siddhartha. They all knew him well. They had played with him at the palace when they were children, and learned how to shoot, fight, and ride together.

**Devadatta** remembered all the times Siddhartha had shot at animals with his bow and arrow and missed. In fact, he couldn't remember his cousin ever killing *anything*!

Arjuna could recall how often Siddhartha fell behind while riding. It never occurred to him that the gentle prince might have felt sorry for his mount, and didn't want to make him work so hard.

Nanda had practiced swordsmanship with Siddhartha once or twice, and noticed that he never fought very hard. Siddhartha didn't have the anger and fury that made a fighter great.

By the time the day of the tournament arrived, the roads for miles around Kapilavastu were clogged with people walking, or riding in bullock carts, rickshaws, litters, and on horses. Everyone, it seemed, wanted to see the contest for Yasodhara's hand.

The princess herself arrived in a litter—a tent made of satin cloth, resting on two long poles and carried by four servants. Her father, too, came to see the young suitors compete. His litter was even grander than his daughter's.

Lord Shuddhodana greeted them both and seated them beside him and Lady Japiti in the grandstand overlooking the field.

The four young contestants entered one at a time. Each was dressed in fine robes and sat upon a magnificent horse. A bow was strung over each man's shoulder, and a sword hung from each one's belt.

Siddhartha entered last, riding on the back of his wonderful white horse, Kantaka. He was the youngest of them all, having just turned seventeen. He was tall and strong, but so were the others—and they looked much tougher and meaner. The crowd gasped at the sight of the prince on his magnificent mount, then let out a great cheer for their hometown hero.

Princess Yasodhara felt her heart leap. She hoped with all her being that Siddhartha would win and become her husband. She was already deeply in love with him and she dreaded being married to any of the others, for she could never hope to love them in the same way.

The first of the three tests was the archery contest. Huge drums with leather skins were set up at the far end of the field. Legend says they were a mile and a half from the archers, and perhaps they were. At any rate, they were a great distance away.

First up were Nanda and Arjuna. They both hit the drumskins right in the center, drawing cheers from the crowd. Then Devadatta stood up.

The crowd held its breath. Could he do better—he, whom everyone said was the greatest archer of all the young men in the region?

Devadatta drew his huge, heavy bow and feathered an arrow into it. Then he turned to the judges. "Those skins are too close," he said. "Place them one hundred yards farther away."

The judges did so. Devadatta shot his first arrow, and it split Nanda's in two! His second shot did the same with Arjuna's.

The crowd went wild. Devadatta had done the impossible. Surely he would win the hand of Yasodhara!

The princess let her sari fall over her face to

hide her tears. She, too, believed she was doomed to marry Devadatta.

Ah, but now it was Siddhartha's turn. He walked straight up to Devadatta and said, "Good shot."

"Ha!" said his cousin. "See if you can beat it."

"I will try," said Siddhartha. "Lend me your bow, will you?"

"This bow?" Devadatta laughed. "You can't handle this bow. It's way too big and heavy for you. You won't even be able to bend it, let alone shoot it!"

He offered the bow. Made from the trunks of three young trees, it was tied with ox tendons and strung with a silver cord.

Siddhartha placed just the tips of his fingers on the cord and drew it back with ease—so far back that the tips of the bow touched. "This bow of yours is nothing but a toy," he said. "Doesn't anyone here have a real man's bow?"

"Are you serious?" Devadatta said.

The chief judge cleared his throat. "Uh,

there is one old bow, which has been stored away for years in the basement of the temple because no one could bend it. They say it belonged to the king of the original Aryan invaders. It was your grandfather's, Siddhartha, but he never used it."

"Well, bring it here at once!" Siddhartha ordered.

The bow was thick with inlaid jewels and was black with age. It was so big and heavy, it made Devadatta's bow look tiny by comparison.

Siddhartha admired it. "With such a bow as this, I will fire a shot worthy of Princess Yasodhara." He turned to the judge. "Now place the target so far away that we can just see it on the horizon."

"But—but My Lord—"

"No buts."

"Are you sure?"

"I'm sure."

Legend says that the drum was placed a full six miles away. Perhaps it was less, perhaps not, but surely it was farther than anyone believed possible to reach. Yet reach it Siddhartha did—his arrow pierced the drumskin right in its center and kept on going until it landed at the base of a mountain. (Today, some people say the arrow pierced the rock and made water flow, creating a small spring that pilgrims still come to see!)

The crowd roared its approval, and the sound was like thunder.

"This is not over yet," Devadatta said with a scowl. "There are still two events to go."

Next up was swordsmanship. With one slash of his saber, Nanda cut through a young tree that was six fingers wide. Arjuna was next. He demanded a tree that was one finger wider, and sliced through that.

"Find me a tree three fingers wider yet," said Devadatta. He knew he had to win this event if he hoped to win the overall contest, and the hand of Yasodhara. With a mighty swing of his saber, he cut the tree in two.

"Ha!" he yelled. "Take that!" He smiled at

Siddhartha. "See if you can cut one thicker than that!"

Siddhartha walked over to the grandstand and said to his father, "Father, give me the ceremonial sword you are wearing."

"This one?" Shuddhodana said. "Why, this is not for slicing things. It's just for decoration, son. It would shatter if you tried to cut a tree with it!"

"Nevertheless, let me have it, please."

Taking the sword, Siddhartha walked over to a tree with twin trunks, each as thick as the one Devadatta had felled. With one move so fast that most people in the crowd saw only a blur, Siddhartha sliced right through both trunks!

So clean was his cut that for a moment, nothing happened. "Ha!" Nanda laughed. "Looks like you lost this time."

"How did you expect to cut through such a tree with a sword like that?" Arjuna asked.

"Oh well, too bad," Devadatta said. "Looks like I've won this part of the tournament."

Just then, a breeze blew across the field. Not a strong one, just a gentle, cool whiff of air. But it was enough to send both tree trunks crashing to the ground. Siddhartha smiled at his rivals. "Shall we go on to horsemanship?" he asked.

In this last event, Siddhartha easily came out on top. Riding, jumping, prancing—Kantaka was so magnificent that the others didn't stand a chance.

"That's no fair!" Devadatta yelled as Siddhartha dismounted. "With a horse like that, it's not an equal contest. We should all be tested on the same animal!"

The chief judge started to argue with him, but Siddhartha stopped him with a gentle hand on his arm. "It is all right," he said. "I don't want anyone to think I won the hand of Princess Yasodhara by cheating. Please bring another horse."

The horse they brought was an untamed wild stallion—a huge, fearsome beast. In the grandstand, King Suprabuddha turned to

Lord Shuddhodana and nodded. "Whoever can ride this beast is worthy of my daughter's hand," he said, "for surely, only the manliest of men can tame the monster."

Neither Nanda nor Devadatta could manage to stay atop the horse for more than a few moments. Arjuna, whom everyone knew was a master horseman, managed to ride him twice around the field before the horse bit Arjuna's ankle and threw him to the ground.

It then reared up, intending to stomp him to death, but the grooms and servants managed to grab the reins and drag the horse away, long enough for Arjuna to escape with his life.

The crowd moaned, and many shouted to Siddhartha, urging him not to risk his life trying to tame such a dangerous beast. Princess Yasodhara once again lowered her sari over her face, unable to watch.

But Siddhartha was not afraid. Slowly, calmly he walked straight up to the horse. While the grooms strained at the ropes, trying to keep the raging animal from attacking the prince, he put one hand over the horse's eyes. "Release him!" he ordered.

The grooms looked at one another, afraid to let go.

"I said, release him!"

Shutting their eyes in fear, the grooms let go. As they did, Siddhartha stroked the horse with his free hand and whispered into its ear, "Do not be afraid, dear one. I mean only to ride you this once, and never again."

The horse whinnied softly, then licked Siddhartha's hand as the crowd gasped in amazement.

Siddhartha now leaped onto the horse's back. Guiding it only with his knees, he rode it around the field, the horse prancing calmly as though it had been ridden by men all its life.

The crowd could no longer contain itself. "Siddhartha has won!" they cried. "There is no one more worthy of the princess!"

King Suprabuddha turned to his daughter. "Yasodhara," he said, "does Prince Siddhartha meet with your approval?"

Yasodhara lifted her veil and smiled brightly.

"Ah, I see that he does." The king turned to Shuddhodana. "Cousin, we have a match. Let the wedding be prepared!"

# CHAPTER FIVE
# A GOLDEN CAGE

Their wedding was the most elaborate anyone in those parts could remember. Astrologers read the stars to set the luckiest wedding date. Musicians came from hundreds of miles away. Dozens of dancing girls, exotic food and drink, and above all, the happy bride and groom.

At the celebration toast, Lord Shuddhodana announced, "It is time to present you with your wedding gift! I have had three palaces built just for you—one for each season of the year. In winter, you will be warm and snug, for there are many fireplaces. In summer, your palace offers refreshing pools and gurgling fountains. Walls of marble will keep it cool and pleasant. And in rainy season, a palace lit with many candles and oil lamps—so that your life is bright and cheerful!"

The guests all marveled at Shuddhodana's generosity. But what he did not mention—not then, not yet—was that all three palaces were placed within the same giant park, and that the whole park was surrounded by three sets of thick, high walls to keep the world out, and his son within. None could enter except by showing the seal of Lord Shuddhodana.

Inside the walls, the three palaces and their grounds were filled with every delight and pleasure. They were very like a gigantic golden cage in which to keep a young man who might very likely fly away one day.

Siddhartha and Yasodhara enjoyed their life together and were very much in love. Never had the young prince seemed so contented. Less dreamy than usual, he took an interest in the magnificent entertainment his father always provided.

But as the years went by, it was clear that

Shuddhodana's strategy could not work forever. Gradually, little by little, Siddhartha fell into dreaming and sighing again. He began ignoring the musicians who played beautiful music all day long, the jugglers and dancing girls, poets, singers, and magicians who performed for him every night.

His love of nature remained. He and Yasodhara would often stroll the great park together, and he sometimes rode Kantaka through the forests and grasslands within the walls.

But he always wondered what was on the other side. Once, when a young singer played a song for him about faraway lands, he stopped her and asked if she had been to those places.

"I have been to some of them, My Lord," she replied shyly.

"Are they as strange and wonderful as the song says?" he asked. "Tell me the truth—I must know!"

"My Lord, you have every sort of wonderful

thing here at home," she said softly, looking down at the floor.

"Do not be afraid," he said soothingly. "Tell me. It is all right."

"Well, it is true that these places are full of amazing sights and things that are new to us. Everything in the world is there. People from many different lands, with all sorts of strange customs. Beautiful palaces and temples."

"I must see these places!" Siddhartha said. "I must travel beyond the walls of this golden prison my father has made for me!"

He went to Lord Shuddhodana and begged to be allowed to venture outside for an excursion. But his father refused.

"But why? Why must I always remain at home?"

"You are too precious to me, and to your people, Siddhartha. Someday you will be a great king—ruler of Sakya and many lands beyond. Until you are ready, you must remain protected."

"Well, when will I be ready, Father? I am twenty-one years old. Am I not a man now?"

It was no use. His father would not say anything more. In truth, he knew that sooner or later, Siddhartha must be allowed to go out into the world and get to know his land and his people.

But not yet. Not until Shuddhodana could be sure his line would live on. Not until Siddhartha and Yasodhara had a child—a son who would carry on the Gautama name if Siddhartha ever did leave the throne to seek holiness and enlightenment.

Years more went by, and still there was no child. Shuddhodana grew more and more worried. He was getting old and knew he would not live many more years. He wished his son would begin to fulfill his promise. He was afraid that Siddhartha would not become a great king in time for him to see it.

Finally, when Siddhartha was twenty-eight, Yasodhara found that she was going to have a child. All of Sakya rejoiced—most of all, Lord Shuddhodana. And when the Brahmins looked Yasodhara over and announced that the baby would be a boy, Shuddhodana was happier still.

Surely, now that he was to have a child, Siddhartha would begin to take seriously his future as Lord of Sakya. But Shuddhodana also realized that it was time at long last for Siddhartha to see his country and its people firsthand.

So when Siddhartha pleaded yet again, for the hundredth time, to be allowed outside the walls of his park and palaces, Shuddhodana finally said, "Yes."

Siddhartha was overjoyed and excited—happier than he had been since winning the famous tournament, and Yasodhara's hand, all those years before.

At last he would begin to see the world. He was confident that once he went out, and came back again safely, his father would allow him more such trips.

Finally, he would escape his golden cage!

But Lord Shuddhodana had not changed his stripes overnight. He was still mightily worried about Siddhartha. He remembered the sages' prophecy: If his son ever saw the sufferings of the real world, he would give up the life of a future king, put on the beggar's robes of a holy man, and leave his kingdom behind.

*Well,* thought Shuddhodana, *there is no way I am going to let that happen.* As he had done many years ago, he ordered that all of Kapilavastu was to be swept completely clean. Every house was to be freshly painted, and the whole city was to be cleared of beggars, sick people, the lame, and the old. There were to be no funerals, or burning of the dead (which is how they dispose of dead bodies in India to this day).

"Nothing must disturb the young prince, or darken his day out on the town," Shuddhodana ordered. "Let my son return home, saying, 'Kapilavastu is like a heaven on Earth!'"

The great day arrived. Prince Siddhartha dressed himself in a splendid outfit of gold cloth and a bejeweled turban. Kissing his pregnant wife farewell, he went outside, where he waited for Channa, his groom, to saddle up Kantaka and harness him to the chariot.

The two rode together, master and groom, with Channa holding the reins. That way, Siddhartha could grab the railing with one hand and wave to his adoring public with the other.

Every man, woman, and child in Kapilavastu came out to get a look at the young prince, their future ruler—all, of course, except for the old, the lame, and the sick.

Siddhartha's reputation had come before him. The people had heard what a wonderful young man he was, and all were eager to see him. They cheered wildly as the procession wound its way down the main street to the square at the city's heart.

From there, they made their way through the great bazaar, past the mansions of the rich Brahmins and Kshatriyas. In the bazaar itself, luxury goods from all over the world were sold.

Spices from Serendib, silks from China, carpets from Persia and Kashmir. Here were the stores of the great merchants: the Vaisyas. Sudra workers, and even the lowly untouchables, had bathed and dressed in their holiday best to greet the prince—from a distance, of course.

"It is truly a wonderful city," said Siddhartha to Channa as they continued down the flower-strewn streets, looping back toward the main square.

Suddenly, as they passed a building painted bright blue (all the buildings looked so bright and fresh!), something—no, some*one*—stumbled out of a doorway and into the street, right in front of Siddhartha's chariot.

*A man!* Siddhartha realized—but what kind of a man was this? The prince had never seen anyone like him before.

His hair was white. His face was a mass of wrinkles, and only three teeth were left in his mouth. His eyes were sightless and clouded over. One of his arms was withered, and the other held a walking stick to help him keep upright. He wore only a ragged, dirty loin-cloth, and his ribs stuck out under the sagging skin of his chest.

"Alms!" the man shouted. "Please, help a poor man buy something to eat! Alms! Alms!"

A terrified gasp went up from the crowd. They quickly surrounded the man and dragged him back inside.

But not before Siddhartha had gotten a good look at him. "That man!" he said. "Channa, what is wrong with him?"

"Wrong with him, My Lord?" Channa replied, looking away, as if searching for some-place to hide. "Why, nothing is wrong with him."

"Nothing! How can you say that? Didn't you see him? He was all stooped over, and he seemed so weak. His eyes were all runny and clouded over, and his skin was so shriveled and wrinkled."

"Nothing is wrong with him, My Lord. It is just that he is very old."

"Old?"

"Yes—he has lived for many, many years. Sixty, maybe seventy or even eighty."

"But why is he so pale and wrinkled? Why do his eyes not see? Why does he stoop over and stumble along? My father is old. His sages are old too—some of them have white hair, it is true, but none of them are so bent and shriveled. Surely there must be something else wrong with this fellow!"

"No, sire," said Channa. "It is true that my lord your father is healthy. His skin glows and his eyes are bright. That is because he is rich, and well fed, and has not had to do hard labor all his life. The same is true for the Brahmins, his wise men, and all the older nobles you see around the palace. Their easy life has kept them in good condition. But someday, sooner or later, they too, will be as this man is. All of us will."

"You mean, this will happen to all people?"

"If they are lucky enough to get old, yes."

"Lucky! You call that lucky?"

"When he was younger, My Lord, he stood as straight as you or I. His skin glowed with youth and health. But over the course of many years, slowly, time took its toll on him."

"And this is what we *all* must look forward to?"

"Er . . . yes, My Lord."

"Even myself and Yasodhara? And our baby that will soon arrive?"

"I am sorry, but it is so. You were not supposed to see it, My Lord." Channa sighed. "It just . . . happened, and the truth can no longer be hidden from you."

Siddhartha was too stunned to reply. In an instant, his life had shifted, as though struck by a great earthquake. The peaceful look that had always been in his eyes vanished, replaced with the knitted brows of worry and pain.

"All my life I have seen only good and beautiful things," he said, staring at the colorful, dancing crowd. "But now I see that not everything is good and beautiful."

"No, My Lord," Channa agreed, looking at

his master with fear in his heart. His job had been to make sure the prince stayed happy—and he had failed!

"Turn the chariot around and take me home," Siddhartha ordered. "I have seen enough. All this beauty and wonder now leaves me cold. It is all empty in the face of this terrible truth."

# CHAPTER SIX
# LIFE AS IT IS

Siddhartha returned to his palace in a dark mood, troubled to the depths of his soul. He went straight to his room and stayed there for hours, pacing back and forth.

That night, the palace chef prepared his favorite dishes, but Siddhartha ate nothing for dinner. He retired to his room early and did not come out all the next day.

Lord Shuddhodana was summoned and was told what had happened. "You have destroyed me!" he shouted, tearing at his hair. He was furious at Channa, and at all his servants, who had allowed his son to see that which he must never see!

Finally, he saw that it was useless to be angry. What was done, was done. Hoping he could limit the damage, he went to knock on Siddhartha's chamber door.

There was no reply, but he entered the room, anyway. The prince was sitting on his bed, staring into space.

"What has come over you, my son?" Shuddhodana asked. "Why do you not eat? Why are you so unhappy?"

"I wish to go out again and see life as it really is," said the prince.

Lord Shuddhodana had succeeded for twenty-nine years in hiding the cruelty of the world from his son's eyes. But now that Siddhartha had seen something of harsh reality, it would be harder than ever to keep him satisfied within the palace walls.

"But you've just returned from a wonderful day in the city!" he said, trying to cheer him up. "Why not rest for a while before going out exploring again?"

"I don't want to rest," said Siddhartha. "I've rested all my life. Now I want to go out and see things—all of Sakya, and the lands beyond!"

"Now, now, let's not get carried away!" Shuddhodana said. "You are young, and must still be guided by me. I am your father and I know what's best for you."

"I must go out again, Father," Siddhartha insisted.

"Mmm. Very well, you shall, my boy," said his father. "I will arrange things, in due time—"

"No! Right away!"

"Right away, then," Shuddhodana said, backing out of the chamber. "Now rest. Your mind is troubled. Sleep will make things right. You'll see—you'll awaken tomorrow morning, and the world won't seem so bleak anymore."

Closing the chamber door, Shuddhodana turned to his servants. "Double the palace guard," he told them, frowning. "See that my son does not go out again."

Siddhartha slept, but his sleep was full of dreams—old people surrounded him, and he recognized their faces: Japiti, his father, Yasodhara . . . Channa . . . even himself!

The morning came, but his old contentment did not return. Only one thought occupied his mind: *Old age comes to all people.*

It would come to him, and to Yasodhara, and to his son who was yet unborn. All, all would someday no longer be young and beautiful, strong and swift. Backs would stoop over, teeth and hair would fall out, skin would sag and shrivel. Every movement would bring pain and suffering.

*It was unbearable! Was there nothing anyone could do about this terrible situation?*

Days passed, and weeks. Soon, his new son would be born—but Siddhartha could not rejoice. What good was it to be born if you had to wither and get old, like that poor man in the street? It all seemed so senseless!

When Siddhartha did not recover from his sadness, Shuddhodana began to despair. He summoned his Brahmins to his side. "What is to be done about the prince?" he asked. "He wants to go out again—and alone, without his retinue and servants!"

"My Lord," said the eldest Brahmin after he and his fellows had conferred among themselves, "perhaps a second trip will undo the damage the first trip has done."

"How so?" asked Shuddhodana.

"When a person steps from darkness into light, they are blinded for a moment. But after a while, their eyes adjust to the light. They can see things as they are, and walk about with confidence. So may it be with the prince. Perhaps, as he gets used to the world outside these walls, he will not be so upset anymore."

Shuddhodana considered this. "It is worth a try," he decided. "I cannot bear the thought of him being this unhappy for the rest of his life."

The next day, Siddhartha once again asked to go out beyond the walls. And this time, his father said yes.

Siddhartha summoned Channa and told him they were going out again.

"Shall I hitch up the chariot, My Lord?" Channa asked.

"No, Channa. Today we will go forth on foot—and in disguise. I don't want everyone we meet to play pretend for my sake. I want them to behave as they would on an ordinary day, not as they do when their prince is present."

And so, the next morning, two men set forth from the gates of the palace, headed for the city. One was dressed as a merchant, and the other as a clerk. Even the palace guards did not recognize them.

For the first time since his last excursion, Siddhartha felt alive—though not happy. He knew there was more he had not yet seen. For twenty-nine years he had lived behind a curtain. Now, the curtain was lifting and he would see life as it really was.

They came into Kapilavastu, unnoticed by anyone. *It was not like the last time I was here,*

Siddhartha thought. It was dirtier, and shabbier. Most people were wearing old clothes, not the brightly colored, brand-new ones they'd had on last time.

Still, it pleased him to see the world as it really was. Here, in the main square, a group of children sat in a semicircle in front of their teacher, or *guru*, learning their lessons, repeating the names of the Brahmanic gods.

There, under a canopy, a blacksmith hammered red-hot metal on an anvil, making swords. Across the square, merchants sold goods, made barrels and brooms and candles. In front of a temple a handsome young couple were getting married by a Brahmin while guests threw lotus blossoms at their feet.

But their joy did not make Siddhartha feel any lighter. "Channa," he said, "tell me this: If we all live only to grow old, and if all beauty is destined to disappear, then how can a person enjoy it? It's like trying to grab the wind—you can't hold on to it, it just keeps blowing. And yet, everyone seems to run after beauty and youth. Don't they see that they can't hold on to it? How is it possible they don't see it?"

Channa was only a humble groom. He had not had a grand education like his master, and did not know how to answer such difficult questions. So he kept silent, but his mind was troubled. Siddhartha was changing before his eyes. Like youth and beauty, the sheltered world of the prince had withered away and could not be put back together.

Still, as the day wore on and they walked the streets of the city, something of its pulsing life, its colors and sounds and smells, the variety of its people, began to cheer Siddhartha. How different from the quiet palace grounds it all was! How very alive!

Suddenly, he froze in his tracks. Not ten feet in front of them, a woman swayed and fell to her knees, groaning and grabbing at the air frantically. She writhed on the ground, drooling, her eyes staring wildly around, her arms and legs thrashing. She shook and quivered, her face twisted in pain. There were spots all over her face and arms, and she was sweating so much, her scarf was soaking wet.

"What is wrong with that woman?" Siddhartha asked, clutching at Channa's sleeve.

"Help me . . . help me . . . ," the woman moaned.

Siddhartha knelt down before her and took her in his arms. "Her skin is burning hot!" he said.

"She is sick with fever, My Lord," Channa replied. "Keep away from her, or you may become sick too!"

Siddhartha did not budge. "What is this 'sick' you speak of? What is 'fever'?"

"It is when your blood boils," said Channa, who certainly did not understand anything about germs (neither did doctors in those days). "Inside, she is rotting away with the illness. It steals her health, and her mind, too. Please, My Lord, let go of her or the plague that ails her may spread inside you as well!"

But Siddhartha would not let go of the

woman. He held her tightly until she stopped shaking and her breathing became peaceful again. She closed her eyes and lay on the ground, breathing deeply, slowly. He took off his turban and placed it beneath her head for a pillow, before rising to his feet.

"Come, My Lord. There is nothing more you can do for her. Time alone can heal a sick person—time and the gods."

"Tell me, Channa," Siddhartha said as they left the square, "this . . . this sickness—this plague, or fever—does it, too, come to all people?"

"Oh no, My Lord!" Channa was happy to say. "It is not like old age, which comes to everyone. If you eat well, and exercise, keep clean, and take good care of yourself, you are likely to remain mostly healthy all the days of your life."

But Siddhartha was not satisfied with this answer. "But that woman is not the only one who is sick, is she? There are many such others, is it not true? Tell me honestly, Channa, for I can be kept in the dark no longer!"

"It is true, My Lord," Channa said, his eyes downcast. "Many people do get sick."

"Even those who take good care of themselves?"

"Sometimes . . . yes . . . even they may get sick. It is like being bitten by a snake. You are walking along and, suddenly, you step on its tail and it bites you. There is no way to avoid what you cannot see coming, My Lord. Sometimes fate strikes a blow, and there is nothing to be done about it."

"So, none of us can go to sleep at night confident he will rise the next morning in good health?"

"No, My Lord."

"I see," said Siddhartha. "And even if we do not get sick, we still must someday grow old and feeble, like that man we saw the last time. Is it not so?"

"It is so, My Lord. If we live that long."

"What is that you say?" Siddhartha asked,

stopping in his tracks. "*If?* What do you mean, *if?*"

Channa had been dreading this question, but he knew that it would come sooner or later and that he would have to answer as best he could. "Some people die before they reach old age."

"Die? What do you mean?"

"All living things must *die* sooner or later, My Lord."

"What? What is this you say?"

Siddhartha was in a complete state of shock. With all his great learning, no one had ever discussed death with him—what it really was, or that it happens to everyone.

"Look, there," Channa said, pointing.

Siddhartha turned and saw a group of people walking down the road in a procession toward the river. In the middle of the procession, carried high on the shoulders of some of the marchers, was an old man on a litter. He lay flat on his back, sprinkled all over with red and yellow powder. His hands were crossed on his chest, and he lay silent and motionless. Everyone else in the group, however, was wailing loudly, tearing at their hair and beating their chests, crying, "Rama!"—calling upon the Brahmanic god of death.

"What is this?" Siddhartha asked.

"This," said Channa, "is a funeral. That old man has died. His life has come to an end, as all lives do."

"What will they do with him now?" asked the prince.

"Come, My Lord, and you shall see."

Channa and Siddhartha followed the procession down to the river. There, the dead man was brought onto a raft and put on top of a pile of sticks. Then a Brahmin set fire to the sticks with a torch, and the raft was set loose onto the river, to float slowly away and be reduced to ashes.

"But . . . but that man will get burned!" Siddhartha cried.

"It does not matter," Channa said. "He will feel nothing. He is beyond all feeling now, beyond joy and suffering."

"How is it he cannot feel, Channa?"

"His soul has already flown, and will be reborn someday. His body will soon return to ashes." Channa sighed. "Not long ago, he was as alive as you or I, working, playing, spending time with his family and friends, listening to music—fully alive. And now . . . ah, well, such is life."

"Is it really so, Channa?" Siddhartha said, his eyes wide, as if seeing the truth for the first time.

"It is, My Lord."

"Then let us return home for now. I must think. I must meditate upon all that I have seen. For the world is not as I have thought until now."

# CHAPTER SEVEN

# A FORK IN THE ROAD

"What is it, my darling? What is wrong?" Yasodhara stroked her husband's hair as they sat together in their chamber. "Why are you so unhappy?"

"Teach me how to be otherwise!" he lamented.

"Why, do you not have everything a person could want? Riches, nobility, youth, beauty, a wife who loves you, and very soon now, a child—a son, if the Brahmins are correct! What reason is there to be glum?"

"Old age . . . sickness . . . death . . . ," said Siddhartha, staring into the darkness.

"That is for later, my sweet—much later. Let us enjoy life and health and youth and riches while we have them!"

"And what of those who don't?" he asked her. "How can I be happy for even a moment when, at that same moment, another living being is suffering?"

"My dear lord," she said, "come and find rest and peace in my arms."

"I cannot, Yasodhara—even your sweet embrace feels hollow, when I think of how someday we shall both grow old and die. This is only a brief, passing moment! Life is heading for death from its very first instant. Even our baby will grow old and die. How can I ever be happy, knowing all this?"

"Be happy in the moment, darling!" Yasodhara pleaded.

"Impossible," he said. "I am living incredibly well, while most people are poor and miserable. Can I ignore their pain and suffering, knowing that someday I, too, will endure the pain of old age and death?"

Yasodhara held him in her arms, saying nothing, for there was nothing more she could say. Nothing anyone could say to the prince could bring him out of his deep sadness.

Siddhartha was only beginning to wrestle with the questions that would occupy his thoughts for the rest of his days until he achieved enlightenment. For now, he only knew that the world outside the palace walls had much to teach him, and that he needed to go out again and learn.

He begged Lord Shuddhodana's permission, since he wanted to remain an obedient son.

"Stay at home, Siddhartha," Shuddhodana begged. "I am afraid for you when you are out."

"Whatever danger is out there, Father, you cannot keep me from it, any more than you can keep me from old age and death."

Shuddhodana sighed. "Long ago, when you were born, the sages said that if you saw human suffering, you would be greatly affected by it. I . . . I only meant to spare you pain."

It was not strictly the truth, for Shuddhodana had other reasons he did not share with his son. But it was true, as far as it went.

"Father, if you will not ever let me go out, then I will flee this place as soon as I can!"

"And where will you go? What will you do?"

"I . . . I do not know, Father," Siddhartha admitted, looking down at the ground. He knew no other life than the one he had lived—but he was certain there was something else, some other path. He only needed to discover it—and he could not do that here.

"All right, my son," Shuddhodana relented. "Since I don't want you thinking of running away from your home, I will allow you to go traveling throughout Sakya again. But allow me to send your teachers and servants with you—you can all make a day of it! A picnic, say, in a grove of beautiful trees . . . yes, that would be fine! With a few dancing girls, and . . ."

"No, Father, I don't want—"

"You want to go out, don't you?"

"Yes, but—"

"Then please, son—be ruled by me. I know what's best for you."

Siddhartha sighed and said, "Very well, Father. Whatever you say."

So it was that he and Channa set out in the chariot, Kantaka proudly prancing before them, with two dozen servants, teachers, and dancing girls bringing up the rear.

Siddhartha was impatient at being followed this way, and once they were out in the countryside beyond the capital, he ordered Channa to go faster. "Leave them in our dust!" he cried. "Let them catch up to us if they can!"

Channa was pleased to see his lord excited and lively again. He flicked the reins, and Kantaka took off at a gallop. The traveling party, riding horses made for carrying burdens, not for running fast, could not keep up.

"I feel like I've been sleeping my whole life long," Siddhartha said as the wind blew back his long, dark hair, "and am only now waking up, for the very first time!"

Before long, they came to a fork in the road. To one side was a large tree, and under it was a man wearing ragged clothing. He sat peacefully, deep in meditation, his legs crossed, his eyes closed, his lips curled in a slight smile of contentment.

"Stop the chariot!" Siddhartha ordered. "What sort of man is this, Channa? I've never seen anyone who looked so deeply happy and at peace!"

"He is a wandering holy man, My Lord—a monk of the forest. Although many such men are Brahmins by birth, they have given up all the things of this world to take up the lives of wandering beggars. These men, called ascetics, separate themselves from all their possessions in hope of achieving Nirvana, the state of permanent enlightenment."

"Ah! Ascetics . . . I did not know such people existed—he is nothing like our sages at the palace."

"No, My Lord. Those Brahmins are rich with the things of this world. This man has said good-bye to all that. He has nothing except a beggar's bowl, a walking stick, and the ragged clothes on his back."

"And yet he looks to be completely free of pain and suffering. He seems so full of kindness and love, such peace and contentment . . . I must speak with him!" Siddhartha got down and went over to the monk, sitting down beside him.

The old man, sensing he had company, opened his eyes. Seeing Siddhartha, he smiled and gave a little nod of his head.

"Greetings, Prince," said the monk. "To what do I owe this honor?"

"Tell me," said Siddhartha, "do all men like you find such perfect peace—for I can see that you have found it."

"Not all," he said. "Not many. But some do. These are called Buddhas. It is said that a Buddha comes along only once in a thousand years." He looked Siddhartha up and down. "Some do," he repeated, his smile growing wider. "Some do. . . ."

There was so much Siddhartha wanted to ask the man, but just then he heard behind him the noise of the caravan catching up to them. The servants and his teachers were all shouting and waving, clearly annoyed at being left behind.

Siddhartha turned back around to continue the conversation, and was astonished to find that the old ascetic had disappeared!

"But—where did he go, Channa? He was here just a minute ago!"

"I don't know, My Lord—I was looking away, just as you were."

Siddhartha shaded his eyes as he stared down both forks of the road, into the far distance. "Where could he have gone?" he wondered aloud. "It's as if he disappeared into thin air!"

The traveling party had caught up to them now. "Come, Prince—let us rest now that you have tired us out so! We will set up our camp in yonder grove of trees, and have our lunch and some entertainment."

Siddhartha allowed himself to be led to the grove. While the others set up carpets and cushions and brought out food and drink and musical instruments, he wandered into a nearby field, where a plowman was driving his oxen, tilling the earth, turning it over so it would be ready to plant.

Siddhartha remembered the time from his childhood when he had gone out into the countryside for the first time, in the chariot with his father. He remembered how the plow had cut the worm in two; how the worm had been eaten by the little bird, and the bird in turn killed and eaten by the eagle.

He felt again the pain of the worm, the agony of the little bird. He remembered his own hurt as he felt in his heart the hurt of other creatures, and realized for the first time how cruel nature could be.

Life ate life, and life followed life in an endless, painful wheel of sorrow! It could not be true—there had to be a way out.

He remembered how, after seeing these things for the first time, he had sat and fallen into a trance. He recalled now that wonderful, peaceful feeling he had then.

With the memory washing over him like a waterfall, he sat himself down against a nearby tree trunk, crossed his legs, and closed his eyes. Just as the wandering monk had done, Siddhartha tried to concentrate on his breathing.

Soon, he fell into a deep meditation—a trance filled with peace and light. In this condition, he felt finally free of the everlasting wheel—free of care, free of pain, free of attachment.

He opened his eyes, still filled with the blissful feeling. And though it disappeared after a few hours, Siddhartha was sure he could make it last longer if he practiced more often. For surely this was the life he had been searching for, ever since that day in Kapilavastu when he saw the old man stumble out of the doorway and into the street.

Two roads now stood before him, forking off in different directions. One road led to riches and power; the other, to poverty and homelessness . . . and maybe, just maybe, to true enlightenment.

\* \* \* \*

Lord Shuddhodana was beside himself with worry. None of his careful precautions had kept Siddhartha from seeing how the world suffers. His son no longer showed any interest at all in being a great ruler of men. Even the prospect of having a son seemed to give him no joy at all.

"We shall name him Rahula," Siddhartha had decided.

"Rahula? But that means 'a bond that ties you down'!" his father complained.

"Exactly—for that is just what he will be to me. Just as you all are. My affection for you will cause me pain whenever any of you suffer. The more I love all living things, the more I must suffer along with them, at every moment!"

Such words made Lord Shuddhodana fear for his son's future. He was sure that if the prince left the palace again anytime soon, he would never return.

"Let the guard be doubled," Shuddhodana ordered, "so that Siddhartha remains at the palace until his son is born. Perhaps when he sees . . . Rahula . . . it will lighten his mood. Babies can have that effect on a parent."

The guard was doubled, and within a week, Yasodhara announced that the time of her labor was near. As was the custom in Sakya and the surrounding kingdoms, the women retreated to their parents' homes to give birth, and so it was with her. She traveled to King Suprabuddha's palace.

It was while she was gone that Siddhartha made his final decision to leave the royal life behind. His life had been happier than any man's until now—and yet, what good was the sort of happiness that ended in old age, sickness, and death? What good was loving people if you had to lose them in the end?

No, it was only perfect happiness that mattered—the kind that would never disappear. Yasodhara always said he should ask the Brahmins about it, but he knew that no Brahmin, no priest, could help him find it. It was the ascetic he'd seen whose face he remembered—the face of perfect happiness.

*The face of freedom from all attachments.*

In order to find that happiness, Siddhartha knew he would have to free himself from everything and everyone he knew, for they were the ties that kept him from reaching enlightenment.

No god or priest would show him the way. He would find that old ascetic—or another—or find it for himself if he had to. Somehow, he would become a Buddha—and when he found the way out of suffering, he would share it with the whole wide world!

When Yasodhara returned to Sakya with her new baby, a huge celebration was already underway. All of Kapilavastu was ablaze with the light of torches as acrobats, magicians, dancers, and singers performed for the happy public.

At the palace, too, the party was in full swing. Everyone was in a grand mood, for soon, Rahula—the baby prince who would someday rule Sakya after his father and grandfather—would be shown to one and all.

Everyone was happy, and drank a lot of wine to celebrate. Everyone, that is, except Siddhartha.

The new father seemed bored with it all. He did not touch his food, drank no wine, and just lay on a cushion, staring at the merriment as though it were taking place a thousand miles away. So distant was he that, after awhile, in spite of the noise and music, he fell fast asleep, right in the middle of the party.

Many of the guests laughed and pointed at the sleeping prince. "He's been up late, not able to sleep, waiting for his wife and child to return," they all told one another with winks and nods.

Of course, they knew nothing of the real reason the prince was so weary. They went on partying and drinking until, one by one, they too began to nod off to sleep. The beautiful dancing girls, the musicians, the jugglers and magicians, seeing that all the guests were sleeping, decided to rest as well. They were tired from all their labors, and many of them had also helped themselves to lots of wine. Why not? After all, it was free!

Siddhartha awoke with a start. He must have been sleeping for hours, for it had been daylight still, and now it was dark night. The torches had burned low, and the only sounds were the grunts and snores of the sleeping guests and performers.

He got to his feet and looked around. How ugly they all looked in their cockeyed sleeping poses. Drooling, that one! Snoring like a pig, that other one! See how the beauty of the dancers' faces was all an illusion of makeup and glitter!

Humanity seemed utterly horrifying to him. He looked at all these young, healthy, contented people, and behind the fullness of their flesh, he saw only the hollow shadows of sickness . . . the withering of old age . . . and, in the end, the skulls and bones and ashes of death.

"I must get out of here," he muttered to

himself. He felt as if there were no air in the great hall, as if he would suffocate if he did not get away from this place!

But he could not leave—not yet. Not without seeing his wife once more, and his baby son for the first, and perhaps last, time.

He crept into their chamber, careful not to make a sound and risk waking them. The two were huddled together, sleeping peacefully, but the baby was hidden underneath his mother's protecting arm. To see his son, he would have had to risk waking them both—and so he left without saying good-bye, without seeing his son's face.

"Someday," he promised silently as he stood at the open window, "someday, when I have found a way out of all this suffering, I will return and see you both. Then I shall share with you, my loves, all that I have learned."

Then he slipped outside, onto the terrace. He climbed a thick vine down to the courtyard below. How good it was to breathe fresh air again! Softly, he knocked on the door of

Channa's room, next to the stables.

"Who is it?" he heard the charioteer's sleepy voice.

"It is I, Siddhartha," he said. "I want you to saddle up Kantaka for me."

"Now? It's the middle of the night!"

"Exactly," said the prince. "Quietly, now—I don't want anyone to see us leave."

Thinking this was another adventure like the ones they'd been having lately, Channa happily dressed and readied the great horse. Soon, the two of them passed out through the gates of the palace. They walked quietly through the empty streets of the city—here too, it seemed, everyone was asleep. It was as though some god had frozen the world so that they could escape unnoticed.

They reached the Anoma River at dawn. It wasn't much of a river, really. At this time of year, a person could wade across it easily. Yet this was the border of Sakya and the Kingdom of Magadha.

When he crossed the river, Siddhartha would

be entering foreign territory for the first time.

"We can go no farther, My Lord," said Channa. "It is time for us to turn back now."

"I am not going back, Channa," Siddhartha said, dismounting and handing Channa the reins. Then, removing all his jewelry, he gave it to his stunned groom. "Tell them all that I am sorry to leave them, Channa—for I love each of them dearly. But if I am to find a way to end the suffering of this world, I must go forward alone from here on."

Channa had heard of the prophecies about Siddhartha—that one day he would give up the life of a king for that of a holy man—but he had never taken them seriously. Who in his right mind, he thought, would want to give up so much wealth and power, and a life of such luxury and pleasure, just to become a beggar?

He gazed at his master, who was now just a silhouette in front of the rising sun. The glow of the sun's rays seemed to sprout from Siddhartha himself, as if he were a god.

"Good-bye, Channa," said the prince. "Good-bye to you, too, Kantaka—my faithful horse. Believe me, I would not leave you all if it were not so very important."

Channa turned to go, crying bitterly. As for Kantaka, he refused to leave the prince's side. The horse loved his master so much that his heart was breaking. Indeed, he had to be dragged back to Kapilavastu by Channa. (Soon afterward, according to legend, Kantaka lay down in his stable and died of grief.)

Siddhartha watched the two of them disappear over the hill. Turning back to the river, he realized he was not alone. A poor beggar sat crouched by the riverbank, an alms bowl in front of him.

Siddhartha had nothing to give him—or did he? "I have no further use for these fine silken robes," he said. "Will you give me yours in exchange?"

The beggar could hardly believe his good luck! He traded clothes with Siddhartha and was busy admiring himself when the prince addressed him again. "Lend me your knife, will you? Just for a moment?"

Taking the knife, Siddhartha cut off his long hair, worn wrapped around his head in the style of a nobleman. "Here," he said, returning the knife to its owner. "Thanks, and good luck to you."

"Thank *you*!" the beggar replied, gathering up Siddhartha's discarded hair. "It will make for fine pillow-stuffing!" he added before going on his way.

Alone now, and dressed in beggar's rags, Siddhartha turned toward the rising sun, toward the new day. He was no longer Prince Siddhartha Gautama. He was no longer a prince at all.

He was Gautama the beggar; Gautama the Boddhisatva—one who seeks Buddhahood. Taking a deep breath and letting it out, he began wading across the river.

## CHAPTER EIGHT
# GAUTAMA THE BEGGAR

Across the river, in the Kingdom of Magadha, Gautama the beggar came to a mango grove. There he sat and meditated for a full seven days, without ever rising to eat or drink. When he finally rose from his trance, he felt wonderfully peaceful and free.

Still, he was a man, and naturally, he was hungry and thirsty. There was no one here to beg from, but there was a brook nearby with fresh water—and plenty of mangoes to eat. He ate and drank his fill—but no more—then continued on his way.

He soon met the hermit Bhagava, a holy man who had advanced quite far along the road to enlightenment. Guatama camped near him and stayed for several days, carefully watching everything the hermit did. But although Bhagava seemed to know many divine secrets, he did not know how to share any of them. And so once again, Gautama continued his wanderings.

Along the road, he met many people. None recognized him as the famous Prince Siddhartha of Sakya, who had won the fabled marriage tournament, and for whom such a wonderful future had been predicted. To them, he was just a wandering beggar from the Gautama clan, a very large and powerful Kshatriya family with hundreds of members.

Several of his roadside companions told him about the faraway forest of Uruvela, on the other side of the Kingdom of Magadha, where many gurus (teachers) were said to live. Some of them had schools of their own, called *ashrams,* each with hundreds of students. Gautama resolved to travel to this forest of holy men and find himself a guru.

After about ninety miles, he came to the capital city of Magadha, Rajagaha. He set himself up under a shady tree on a downtown street corner, prepared to beg for his next meal.

At his castle overlooking the town, King Bimbisara of Magadha was brought news of the new arrival to their city. "He is no ordinary ascetic," said Bimbisara's officer. "He looks more like a Brahmin, or a prince."

"What is his name?"

"Gautama, he says."

"Gautama? Hmmm . . . ," Bimbisara said, "perhaps he is that son of my neighbor Lord Shuddhodana. I have heard this young man has left his kingdom to become a holy man."

King Bimbisara considered himself a very religious man. He surrounded himself with lots of Brahmins and gave generously to all kinds of holy men and monks. Because of his generosity, many people tried to take advantage, pretending they were holy men when they really weren't. Bimbisara had become expert at telling the real from the fake.

"We shall see if this fellow is truly someone special," he told his officer. "Get my chariot ready at once!"

Gautama stood on the street corner, holding out his begging bowl. People walked by, staring at him. It wasn't every beggar who stood so straight and tall, who had such noble bearing and features.

A few poor folk approached him, throwing scraps of their own meager food into his bowl. "Thank you," he said to each of them.

When his bowl was full, he sat down on the curb to eat. Stuffing a mouthful between his lips, he nearly vomited. "Augh!" he cried. "This food is disgusting!"

It was like nothing he had ever eaten before. He was about to dump the whole bowl out on the ground when he stopped himself, ashamed.

"Who do you think you are?" he asked himself. "When you ate all that wonderful food back at the palace, didn't you wish to live the life of a beggar? Now that you have what you wished for, just what are you doing? These poor people have given you their humble rations, yet you would scorn their gift?"

He sat back down, and began to feed himself— just a little at a time, so he could begin to get used to it. He chewed each mouthful carefully, paying full attention to whatever taste was there. Soon he began to eat gratefully, happy to be alive and in the moment, with nourishment—however humble—to satisfy his hunger.

At that moment, King Bimbisara's chariot approached. "See how he sits there!" he said to his coachman. "A prince among princes if ever I saw one—yet dressed in beggar's rags and eating happily the leftovers given him by the poorest of the poor."

Bimbisara stepped down from his chariot and approached him. "Who are you, young man?" he asked. "And why have you come to my capital?"

"My name is Gautama," said Siddhartha, "and I have come seeking the wise men of the Uruvela forest. I wish to become a Buddha and

I hope they will be able to guide me in my quest."

"I know exactly who you are," said Bimbisara. "Tell me, Prince Siddhartha, why have you left Sakya? Did you have a fight with your father?"

"No . . . nothing like that."

"It is not right for a man like you, of such grace and nobility, to give up everything for the life of a wandering beggar."

Guatama did not answer. He only looked humbly down at the ground.

"Perhaps you would like it better here," Bimbisara went on. "I have no son of my own, you know. Would you perhaps agree to stay here and help me rule Magadha in my old age? You could have half my kingdom if you would only stay!"

"I cannot . . . I'm sorry . . ."

Seeing that the young man was determined to pursue his quest, the king tried one more tactic. "You know, I am a great patron of holy men. I would be happy to provide you with a lovely park to live and meditate in, if you'll stay here in Rajagaha and help me rule my kingdom justly."

"My Lord, I have already left my own kingdom, and I have no wish to rule another. I am seeking the kind of happiness that does not depend on the daily events of life. I only wish to become enlightened and to share what I discover with the whole world."

When King Bimbisara saw that he could not make the young man change his mind, he was impressed. "I am sure you will succeed in your quest," he said. "And when you do, please promise to return here and teach me what you have learned. Make me one of your very first pupils!"

"I promise, My Lord."

The two men bowed to each other in respect and friendship. Bimbisara presented him with the complete requirements of a wandering monk: three orange robes, a wooden alms bowl, a needle, a razor, a water-strainer, and a belt. Gautama accepted the gifts with a bow.

The king got back in his chariot and drove

back to the palace. As for Gautama the beggar, he turned and continued on his way to Uruvela, the forest of the wise men.

Later that day, he was eating his humble meal when five men, wearing the orange robes of fellow seekers, approached him. "Don't you recognize us?" the oldest of them asked him.

"Should I?"

They did look vaguely familiar to him, but he could not place their faces.

"I am Kondanna," said the oldest. "I was the youngest of your father's Brahmin counselors. We were the ones who predicted this quest of yours."

"You predicted that I—?"

"The others insisted on telling your father that you could also become a great king and ruler of men," Kondanna went on. "I objected because I could see only this one path for you. And so I left your father's service and have been a wanderer ever since—lo, these twenty-eight years."

"And these others?" Gautama asked, pointing to the four younger men who surrounded Kondanna.

"They are the sons of four of the other counselors," Kondanna explained. "This is Bhaddiya, and Vappa, Mahanama and Assaji. We have been together for many years now, seeking enlightenment. Now that you, too, are on that path, we will follow you wherever you go—for I am sure you are destined to achieve Nirvana."

"I'm glad you think so," said Gautama, smiling. "I hope you are right—and you are most welcome to come with me."

"Where are you going?" Kondanna asked.

"To Uruvela."

"Which guru will you choose?"

"Well, I have heard of a Brahmanic sage by the name of Alara Kalama. He has many students, and everyone speaks well of him."

The five orange-robed companions walked with him the rest of the way to the Uruvela forest, where Alara Kalama had his ashram, or school. Gautama asked to be taken in as a student along with his friends, and the six were accepted.

"My doctrine is so simple that in no time at all, an intelligent man can grasp its essence and use it to teach himself the rest," said the great guru.

Gautama took his teacher's words to heart. And indeed, after only a few months, he found that he completely understood the basic principles of Alara Kalama's teaching.

Immediately, he went to see his guru and told him this. Alara Kalama gazed deeply into his student's eyes. He quizzed him in his understanding, and soon realized that Siddhartha had indeed absorbed his whole teaching. "Now you can help me run the ashram!" said the teacher. "You and I will lead it together!"

"I am sorry, *Rishi*," said Guatama, "but I must go farther in my search for Nirvana. I must now seek other teachers to help me reach that incomparable, peaceful state."

He left the ashram, taking his five companions with him. Together, they sought out another guru of the forest, Uddaka Ramaputta, who taught a doctrine leading to a realm of "perception and not-perception."

Once again, after only a few months, Guatama found he had learned all that he could from his teacher. It was the same as when he was a child with his tutors. Once again, as before, he went to his guru and explained.

Uddaka Ramaputta, seeing that his pupil had indeed surpassed him, offered him the leadership of his ashram, but Gautama refused.

That night, the future Buddha sat up late under the stars with his five companions and announced that he was once again leaving the ashram.

"We will go with you, wherever you go," said Kondanna, and the others nodded their heads in agreement.

"I am grateful for your loyalty," said Gautama, "but this time, I do not intend to find another guru, nor join another ashram. I intend to live in this forest on my own. I must separate myself from all attachments, and from the material world, as much as possible."

The five companions liked this plan. They all believed that neither guru so far had been demanding enough. They wanted to go much further in denying themselves all pleasures, even food and warmth. "We will be true ascetics, denying ourselves all pleasure, all comfort— even most food and drink!"

The very next day, the six men departed the ashram together. Along their way, Gautama gathered his thoughts. He had begun his quest by trying to learn from Bhagava the hermit, who knew much but could not teach him. He then found two wonderful teachers, but had soon learned all he could from them.

From now on, he knew, he would have to seek enlightenment—Nirvana—on his own. And it would be much harder than anything he had ever done before.

# CHAPTER NINE

# THE MIDDLE WAY

The six companions soon came to the River Naranjana. They were now in the heart of the Uruvela forest. They followed the river to a spot near Gaya town, with its great castle looming over the shore.

Here, there were shady trees to camp under, and many passersby along the river from whom to beg food. Best of all, there was the river itself, with its gurgling and whooshing sounds, and the animals who came to drink from its cool waters.

Here was the perfect place in which to struggle for enlightenment, thought Gautama the ascetic. For it was going to be a mighty struggle—against their own desires and feelings; against fear, anger, envy, and greed.

Here, he would empty his body and soul of the soft life he had led until now. Here, in this peaceful place, he would fight his own demons, trying to break free forever from the bonds of suffering, old age, and death.

For the next five years, the companions lived out in the open, unprotected from the rain, wind, cold, and burning heat. They ate little, often going without food altogether for weeks at a time. And none of them went without food and drink more often than Gautama.

As the years went by, he consumed less and less. First one meal a day, then one meal every two days, then one every three days. When he did eat, it was sometimes as little as a single grain of rice. Then he stopped begging altogether and ate only roots, leaves, and fruit.

Gautama's skin became wrinkled, as dry and thin as paper—so thin, you could almost see right through it. His eyes were sunken into his skull like those of an old, sick man. His bones were like hollow bamboo flutes, brittle and weak. He lived with the intense pain of hunger, day and night.

He practiced holding his breath till he was on the verge of losing consciousness. He bathed in icy water in winter, and sat out all day long in the hottest sun of summer. Time after time, his companions thought he was on the verge of death. Crying and shouting, they begged him to take a little food and drink.

By their sixth year together, even Gautama himself knew that they were right. If he did not attain Nirvana very soon, he would die at his own hand, slowly and painfully—for nothing!

One day, after another long fast, Gautama was bathing in the river, when he suddenly realized that he was too weak to climb out of the water. He grabbed a branch and held on with all his diminished strength, fighting against the current that was pulling him to his death. He realized that he was about to die from weakness brought on by six years of hunger, thirst, and physical punishment.

At that very moment, as he hovered between

life and death, he heard a woman shouting. As he passed out, letting go of the branch and surrendering to his fate, he felt soft yet strong arms underneath him, wrestling him toward the shore.

When he awoke, he was staring into the face of a young woman. "Are you a man, or a god?" she asked him.

"I am a man only—a man in search of the truth. Gautama is my name," he said.

"My name is Sujata," said the young woman. "I came here to offer a gift to the gods, in honor of our firstborn child. It is the finest milk from my husband's cows. When I saw you sitting there, meditating, you were so radiant that I thought you must be a god. And then, when I saw how weak you were—how you couldn't get back out of the water . . . please, sir, take the gift I have brought. Drink it, and restore your strength."

He thought about whether he should accept this gift. For twenty-nine years, he had indulged himself in everything good that life had to offer. Then, for the past six years, he had punished and tortured himself, denying himself every comfort, and even most necessities. But in the end, it was still all about *self*—and so it had all been for nothing!

He could see now that there had to be another way—a middle way—between needless suffering and blind indulgence. He would find that way, and share it with everyone in the world. Gratefully, Gautama accepted the gift of special milk and drank it down.

"Thank you," he told Sujata. "Now I shall surely regain my strength and find the truth I am seeking."

From then on, he would torture himself no more. He would regain his health. He would meditate without stopping, until he finally found the path to enlightenment.

His five ascetic companions, standing not far away, saw everything that had happened. They were shocked and angry that Gautama, who had always denied himself more than any of them, was now accepting rich food to eat—

and from a young woman, no less! It seemed to them that their leader had given up his quest for enlightenment.

"How can we follow him any longer?" they asked themselves. "He has betrayed our hopes and our trust in him. Let us go somewhere else, where we can continue our efforts, free of such corruption and weakness." They agreed to walk to Benares, 140 miles away, where there was a deer park called Rishipatana, well known for harboring holy men like themselves.

Gautama accepted his friends' decision without an argument. He was sad that they had misunderstood him, but he did not try to convince them that they were mistaken. He knew that from then on, he must walk the path to Nirvana on his own. Later, when he found what he was looking for, there would be time enough to find them again and share it with them.

Alone, he remained in the forest of Uruvela. Each day, from sunup to sundown, he sat under the banyan tree on the shore of the River

Naranjana, delving deeper and deeper into his meditations.

Since he was once again accepting donations of food from the local people, he soon got stronger and was able to meditate for longer periods of time. He was less and less tempted by distractions, or by his own inner weaknesses. Soon, he knew, he would reach Nirvana and step off the endless wheel of life, death, and suffering.

The new path he had begun traveling in his meditation was different than anything he had learned with his Brahmin teachers, or practiced with his fellow ascetics. His new path was one of pure compassion.

While he grew less and less attached to all the things of this world, his love for all living things grew deeper and wider. Soon, he began to think of himself as something that included everything in the universe. He was part of the greater whole, and in every grain of his being lived all of creation.

One day, a shepherd passed by the banyan

tree, leading dozens of sheep, lambs, and goats. One little lamb trailed badly behind, limping on an injured leg. Gautama gathered it in his arms and spoke gently to it, calming its fears. Then he went to talk to the shepherd.

"Where are you taking these animals? It's high noon—not the hour for bringing them to the fold."

"I am bringing these animals to a great feast at Rajagaha," said the shepherd. "They are to be sacrificed to the gods!"

Sacrificing animals to the gods was a common practice in those days, but it seemed now to Gautama that killing animals for anything but food was cruel, wasteful, and wrong. He decided to journey with the shepherd to Rajagaha.

There, he stood on the edges of the crowd as the great festival commenced. He saw King Bimbisara, along with his chief Brahmins, getting ready to sacrifice the animals.

At the last moment, Gautama strode forward and said, "Great king! Hear me—do not let them take the lives of these animals!"

There was a great murmur from the crowd, but the king, recognizing him, gave the order to stop the killing.

"On what grounds do you ask me to do this, holy one?" Bimbisara asked. He could see, as could everyone there, that Gautama was no ordinary ascetic. He practically glowed with holiness, even though he was not yet a Buddha.

"These animals look up to us, as though we were gods," Guatama explained. "They depend on us for food, and drink, and pasture, and life itself. They give us gifts of wool and milk, cheese and butter. We repay them very poorly when we take their lives this way."

"But we must please the gods!" Bimbisara pointed out.

"If the gods are good, they will not want us to take life so needlessly," Siddhartha said. "And if they are bad, then the bribe will do you no good. Whereas, if the gods don't exist, all the lives of these poor creatures have been completely wasted!

"Besides," he went on, "if we believe in

*reincarnation,* we must also believe that these animals may become humans in their next life. They, like ourselves, are on the endless wheel of life, death, and suffering. Let us allow them whatever happiness is rightfully theirs in this life. Good causes make good effects. By showing compassion, by sparing these animals' lives, we can earn merit for ourselves in the next life."

King Bimbisara was so moved by Gautama's words that he ordered his priests to put down their knives. Then and there, he issued a decree banning all killing of animals, whether for sacrifice or for meat. "For it is love and mercy, not blood, that will bring mercy upon our own heads," he told his cheering people.

Then he turned to Gautama. "Again I ask you to stay with me, holy one," the king begged. "Teach me all your wisdom!"

"I cannot teach what I still have not understood fully," said Gautama. "When I have found that which I seek, I will return again, and do as you ask." With that, he turned away and left the city, headed back to Uruvela.

★ ★ ★ ★

Gautama felt certain that he was now very close to enlightenment. He found a wild fig tree (also called a bo tree, or *bodhi* tree) at the banks of the Naranjana River. Spreading sacred *kusa* grass—a gift from a local farmer—at the foot of the tree to make himself more comfortable, he sat himself down in the lotus position.

The sun was setting, and the full moon beginning to rise. Siddhartha Gautama looked out at the river, its waters passing steadily by him like the endless cycle of life, and said, "Now, I will meditate until I have reached the other shore. I will not rise to eat or drink, or for any other reason. My bones may break, my flesh may creep, my blood may run thin—but here I will remain, until I have found the path to enlightenment."

Through all his twenty-nine years of luxury and comfort, he had always known that the truth lay elsewhere. For the past six years he had searched in vain for it through self-punishment.

Now, he was sure he had come to the very gates of the truth. Tonight, he would will those gates open with the strength of his mind and spirit.

The moon rose, glittering off the river, creating a halo of brightness around the bodhi tree where the lone monk sat, as still as a stone. It was impossible to tell if he was breathing, but all around him, a holy stillness prevailed. Even the river fell silent as it moved on its endless way.

Inside Gautama's body and mind, however, a titanic struggle was going on. Legend has it that Mara, the king of the Demons, was alarmed to see that this young man was about to discover the universal truth and share it with all humankind. Knowing that this would spell doom for him and all his kind, Mara tried every trick he knew to frighten Gautama away from the gates of truth.

But Gautama could no longer be frightened. He could no longer be tempted, or weakened, or frustrated. With patience, his mind defeated each demon Mara sent, by shining the light of truth upon it.

Perhaps it is only a legend, but how else to make humans understand something of what it must have been like for Gautama that night? For what are demons, really, but our own inner weaknesses, which rise up to frighten or tempt us whenever we try to grow beyond ourselves?

For Gautama, his many years of discipline in meditation, of going without all the good things of this world, helped him greatly that night.

He knew that all human suffering results from our being attached to things—to riches, to fame, to long life, to other people. It is our blindness that makes us unhappy. Not seeing that everything is always changing, and that running after pleasure can only result in disappointment, we create our own misery, our minds filling with greed and hatred.

Gautama also knew that good causes make good effects, and bad causes bad ones, and he knew that there is no enlightenment without compassion for every living thing.

In the end, the legend goes, Mara himself tried to dissuade Gautama. "You think you can succeed, where so many others have failed?" he roared. "Show me a witness who can swear that you are worthy of succeeding!"

Gautama said not a word. He only raised his hand and placed it on the ground before him. It was as if he were saying, "The earth itself is my witness!"

To which Mara could only admit defeat. He disintegrated into nothingness, leaving Gautama alone at last, in front of the open gates.

The moon set, and the sun rose. It was the eighth of December, 528 B.C.

When he arose from his seat beneath the bodhi tree, he was no longer Gautama the beggar. Nor was he Siddhartha the prince.

He was now, and forever afterward, *the Buddha.*

## CHAPTER TEN

# THE FIRST TURNING OF THE WHEEL

"This is my last birth!" he announced to the birds and the tree and the river. "My freedom is assured. There will be no more re-becoming!"

The Buddha then sat and rested for seven days more beneath the bodhi tree. During this time, it is said that Mara once more tried to tempt him, saying, "You may have attained enlightenment, but no one will understand your teaching. You're wasting your time. Why not just die now and reach Nirvana, once and for all?"

"Do you see those lotus flowers at the edge of the river?" the Buddha replied. "Some are so far beneath the surface that they will never reach it and flower. Some have already reached the surface. But a few are still struggling to reach the surface. They still have a chance to bloom.

"So it is with human beings. Most will never reach enlightenment in this lifetime. A few already have, perhaps. The rest are struggling to reach Nirvana. Even if only a few are ready to hear the truth, I will share with them. It will be worth it if I can help even one become enlightened."

Defeated once again, Mara withdrew from the Buddha's presence for the last time.

Soon afterward, two traveling merchants, Tapussu and Bhallika, happened by. They offered the radiant monk a simple meal of barley gruel and honey. As he ate, the Buddha told them something of the Middle Way, and they became his first lay disciples (lay, meaning they continued to live their usual lives instead of living with their master or with other monks).

By the time seven days had gone by, the

Buddha had decided on his next step. In order to share his teaching—the Great Law of the Dharma—with all humankind, he would first need to gather some disciples around him.

These students would become the first monks of his new order: the *Sangha*. It was important that these first few students understand quickly what he had to teach them, so that they could spread the doctrine around the world.

But where could he find such holy men?

He had first wanted to start by instructing his old teachers, Alara Kalama and Uddaka. But Tapussu and Bhallika told him that his old teachers had both died. And so the Buddha decided to go find his old companions, the five ascetics. They had gone off to the Rishipatana deer park near Benares. Very well, he would go there and find them.

It was a hot, dusty morning. The five ascetics had just returned from a nearby village where they had begged their meager daily meal. They were sitting down to eat it, when suddenly, they all fell still at once.

Perhaps it was just something in the air— although there was no wind that day. Or maybe it was that peculiar glow, surrounding the monk who was coming down the path toward them. . . .

"It is Gautama!" Kondanna gasped. "But look how he has changed!"

"Yes," said one of the others. "It must be all that good food he's been eating. Let's ignore him. He's not worth our time."

But these five men were no ordinary men— they had spent years searching for truth and living the lives of holy men. They could see that their one-time friend Gautama had advanced in his quest, to a place far beyond where any of them had gone.

"Brother Gautama!" Kondanna said. "Why have you come seeking us out?"

"I am no longer Gautama," he replied. "Nor am I Siddhartha. I have attained enlightenment and am now a Buddha. I have come to teach you the Middle Way—the Great Law of the Dharma. Will you hear me?"

Forgetting that they had agreed to show him no respect, the five ascetics hurried to make the Buddha comfortable—for they had no doubt that he was telling the truth. One prepared a place for him to sit, another brought water to wash his dusty feet. Then they all gathered around him to hear what would be the Buddha's very first *sutra*, or sermon.

In those days, in other parts of the world, alphabets and pictographs were being used to write down the important thoughts of great teachers. But writing had not yet reached the lands of northern India. And so most teachers there shared their lessons by grouping things in numbers. So it was with the Buddha.

"You should first know," he told his friends, "that in order to understand the Great Law of the Dharma, you must first accept Four Noble Truths:

"The first of these is the Truth of Suffering. Everything in life—birth, old age, sickness, death—brings suffering. We suffer when we do not get what we wish for. We suffer when we *do* get what we do *not* wish for. We suffer when we do not have what is pleasant. Even when we *do* have it, we know we will someday lose it, and this, too, causes us suffering.

"The Second Noble Truth is that of the Cause of Suffering. It comes from craving for things—for long life, for riches, for pleasures and delights, for power.

"The Third Noble Truth is that of the End of Suffering. It ends when we are free of craving, of clinging to desires. We strive to attain this release by giving craving no place in our lives.

"The Fourth Noble Truth is that of the Path to the End of Suffering—that is, the Middle Way.

"Why do I call it the Middle Way? Because this path leads between the pursuit of desires and pleasures on the one hand, and the pursuit of pain and hardship on the other. Both these extremes are unhelpful because they can only result in discontent. But by steering clear of them, we can attain the Middle Way—the path to enlightenment.

"The Middle Way is an Eightfold Path: it consists of Right Understanding, Right Attitude of Mind, Right Conduct, Right Livelihood, Right Speech, Right Effort, Right Attentiveness, and Right Concentration.

"In all these areas, we must strive to avoid the two extremes, remembering the Four Noble Truths. This path will lead to clear vision, wisdom, and peace. Following it, we can attain wholeness, bliss, and, in the end, Nirvana."

The five disciples were astounded by how simple and clear the Buddha's vision was. But they still had questions.

"Tell us, O Buddha," said Kondanna, "how can we truly banish craving from our minds? We have denied ourselves everything these past six years, and yet, we have not attained true enlightenment."

"Desire and craving spring from ignorance," the Buddha explained. "This ignorance makes us weak and blind. We have only to see clearly, and we will be free of craving."

"And how do we do that?" asked another of the five.

"We do it by understanding that nothing is permanent—that everything is always changing. Whatever you can think of, remember that it is only temporary. Say to yourself, 'This is not mine, this is not me, or any part of me.' That goes for your desires, your thoughts, and your feelings. Think of them as bubbles on the surface of a river—here for a moment, then gone forever.

"You are not your body either—your body is simply the space, the house, in which you exist for now."

"Tell us more about the Eightfold Path," said Kondanna.

"Very well. What I mean by Right Understanding is seeing life as it is—in other words, understanding the Four Noble Truths. Right Thought means that we keep ourselves free of harmful thoughts and feelings, like hatred, greed, or envy—those that increase suffering for ourselves or others. Right Speech means that we speak only words that will contribute to universal happiness and help end suffering. There is to be no lying, gossip, or saying mean things about others.

"Right Conduct means that we practice what we preach. It is not good to indulge ourselves in drunkenness or meanness. Right Livelihood means we should not do work that results in suffering, like selling weapons or cheating people—but only do work that increases peace and happiness.

"Right Effort means that we must constantly struggle to free ourselves of cravings, and to see the universe clearly. To that end, we must exercise Right Mindfulness—paying strict attention to everything around us and within us, starting with our own breathing. And that brings us to Right Concentration— the frequent meditation that can help us achieve clear vision, freedom from craving, and ultimate bliss."

Day after day, throughout that rainy season, the Buddha and his five disciples sat in the deer park, meditating and studying the Great Law of the Dharma. Soon, the five ascetics achieved enlightenment themselves, though none had succeeded before hearing the Buddha's teaching.

When spring came and the rains ended, they went out to spread the word that the Buddha had come, bringing with him the new teaching that the world had long been waiting for.

This was a teaching that every person could follow, for it did not rely on a guru to lead one to the truth. The Great Law of the Dharma *itself* was the teacher. And unlike the Brahmanic religion, the Buddha's teaching was available to one and all, regardless of caste— everyone could hope to someday reach enlightenment!

# CHAPTER ELEVEN

# THE SANGHA

First, the Buddha and his five disciples visited the other gurus of Uruvela to tell them of the new teaching. Three of these holy men, who all happened to be named Kassapa, joined the Buddha's new order of monks—the Sangha—with all their followers, numbering well over one thousand.

Local young men, wealthy and bored, came to see this new preacher, and quickly asked to join the group and become monks as well.

Many Brahmins, too, priests of the old religion, found themselves attracted to the Buddha's teachings. They began gathering around him in the Uruvela forest, swelling the Sangha's numbers further.

But it was not only the wellborn who flocked

to the Buddha's new order. Many poor folk came too. These simple people had never understood the Brahmanic religion of the priests.

Having never gone to school, they would never have been able to grasp the Four Noble Truths and the Eightfold Path. So the Buddha taught these seekers not with doctrines and complicated ideas, but with simple lessons that anyone could understand.

One day, for instance, a sobbing woman named Gotami came to see the Buddha, carrying the dead body of a small boy in her arms. "O Blessed One," she said to him, "my little child has just died. Everyone says you are the Buddha. If you are, then please, bring my baby back to life!"

"I can help you," said the Buddha, "if you will first bring me a mustard seed."

"Just one mustard seed?" asked Gotami.

"Yes, but it must be from a household where no one has ever died."

Quickly, the young woman raced off to find such a mustard seed. At the first house where she knocked, she was told, "You can have a mustard seed, gladly, but you must know that my husband died just last year."

Gotami continued on to the next house. "I lost my son two years ago," said the woman who answered the door. So it was at every house where she knocked: Everywhere, someone seemed to have died.

Finally, she returned to the Buddha's encampment.

"What has happened, Gotami?" asked the Buddha. "You are no longer carrying your dead little boy. And where is the mustard seed I sent you for?"

Gotami lowered her gaze to the ground, for she now understood why he had sent her on her impossible quest. "I have found that there is no house, anywhere, where tragedy has never struck. Everyone has lost someone they loved. I am not alone in my sorrow. I have now accepted my boy's death. I laid him on the funeral pyre myself, and set fire to his remains. Now I wish only to study the Great Law of the Dharma."

"You have learned an important lesson, Gotami. We all must die someday, sooner or later—for all things are impermanent. By accepting this fact, you can live your life with happiness and gratitude, and in the end, die content."

The Buddha also taught simple lessons through fables—stories with moral lessons behind them.

One such fable was of the Blind Men and the Elephant. It is famous to this day. You've probably heard it yourself. Here is how it goes:

There was once a king who had five wise men, all of them blind. One day, news came that another ruler had sent the king a gift. It was reported to be a new kind of creature—an elephant—that had never been seen in the kingdom before.

So the king sent his wise men to examine the gift and report back to him whether he should accept it. Each blind wise man examined a different part of the beast. Then they all returned to their king to deliver their report.

The one who had felt the elephant's head said, "An elephant is like a cooking pot." The one who had felt the ear said, "It is like a grain basket." The one who'd felt the tusk said, "It is like a spear." Another who'd felt the leg said, "It is like a pillar!"

"No, it is like a broom!" said he who had felt the elephant's tail.

Soon, the wise men began to argue with one another, and before they knew it, they were punching and kicking one another!

"Stop!" cried the king, who had to laugh in spite of himself. "Since you cannot agree, you must all be mistaken."

"And so they all were," the Buddha then explained. "Each blind man had examined only a part of the whole, yet thought that he alone knew what the whole animal was like. So it is with all people who imagine they understand the whole truth, when all they can really see is a small part of the whole."

* * * *

As great and new as his ideas were, as simple to follow as his fables were, the greatest lesson of the Buddha was his own presence. Just being around him, his followers could see a perfect picture of how to approach life in this world. With him nearby as a living example of enlightenment, it was easy to understand his teaching.

Still, not *everyone* was immediately impressed with the Buddha and his new "Middle Way." A few people even treated him rudely.

One such man said, "You're just a phony, Gautama. Why should I think you're any different from all the others? You're just as stupid as the rest of them!"

The monks of the Sangha were angry with this man, but the Buddha did not get upset. Instead, he asked the man, "If you bought a present for someone, and he refused it, to whom would it belong?"

"Why, to me!" said the rude man. "They

rejected it, so it's mine! After all, I'm the one who paid for it!"

"Exactly," said the Buddha. "And so it is with your anger at me. You offer it to me, but I am not insulted by it—and so it still belongs to you. Tell me, though—why would you want it? Anger can only make you unhappy. Why not stop hurting yourself, by giving up your anger and loving all of creation? This will make you happy, and will bring joy to everyone around you as well."

The man fell to his knees. "Of course! Why could I not see that myself? Please, O Blessed One—be my teacher!"

"Come, then," said the Buddha. "I will refuse no one who seeks to learn what I have to share."

Just as there were those who doubted him, there were others who revered him too much. One day, one of them said to the Buddha: "O Blessed One, you are surely the greatest guru who ever lived!"

"Oh, really?" said the Buddha. "Have you

met them all? Do you know all the gurus who have ever been or ever will be?"

"I . . . I . . ."

"It is foolish to say I am the greatest guru. You cannot possibly know that this is true."

"But your teachings have been so much help to me! I only wanted to shout your praises to the skies!"

"Then devote your energies to practicing what I have taught you," said the Buddha. "Do not waste your time praising me—my only purpose here is to teach people. Therefore, practice harder and you will please me more than with all this lavish praise."

Like Brahmanism before it, Buddhism featured the idea of *Karma*—that everything we do or think has an effect, good or bad. Therefore, it is best to think and act well, so that more good things may result.

But unlike Brahmanism, which was so exclusive, the Buddha's new Middle Way welcomed *everyone*.

One day, the monks of the Sangha (many of them Brahmins themselves) were walking down the street when they happened upon an "untouchable"—Sunita by name. Sunita was a garbage-picker, cleaning the streets and selling what scraps could be sold. It was a job that no one of any caste would have accepted.

When Sunita saw the party of monks, most of them high-caste, he tried to escape their notice so that they would not be dirtied by looking at him. He could not get away in time, though. So he flattened himself against a wall, bowed low, and put his hands together in respect.

Imagine his surprise when he looked up to see the leader of the monks coming straight for him! "Please, sir, do not beat me!" Sunita begged. "I did not mean to contaminate you with my presence!"

The Buddha smiled at him kindly and touched him on the shoulder. "Would you like to give up your job and join us? I will teach you the way to reach enlightenment."

Then and there, Sunita dropped his sack of garbage pickings and joined the Sangha. At first, many of the Brahmins were uncomfortable with his presence among them, but after a while, as more untouchables joined the group, they became used to it and saw that the compassion of the Buddha was better than separation by caste, which could only bring suffering.

One day, the Buddha called his closest followers to him and said, "It is time I kept my promise to King Bimbisara, and returned to teach him the Great Law of the Dharma. Let us go now to Rajagaha, before the next rainy season sets in."

By this time, the Sangha numbered well over a thousand monks and lay followers. And so it was quite a procession that made its way toward Magadha's capital city. Messengers brought word to the king of the party's approach.

"Where are they now?" Bimbisara asked.

"They are encamped just outside the city

gates, sire—in the bamboo grove at Vulture's Peak."

"Why, that's my pleasure garden! An excellent spot indeed. Prepare my carriage and my royal guard. And summon my Brahmins. I want them to accompany me so that I may see them argue religion face-to-face with my friend Gautama."

Bimbisara rode off at the head of a large honor guard to visit his guest. As they approached the bamboo grove, the king saw that there were thousands of people camped there, including many from Rajagaha itself.

And yet, Gautama had only been here for one day! So fast did news travel along the roads—and such was the reputation of this one-time prince they were now calling the Buddha.

Bimbisara was stunned to see Kassapa of Uruvela in the crowd. "Has he, too, become a follower?" he gasped. For he had met this great sage, and knew him to be a very holy man. If even Kassapa had acknowledged Gautama as the Buddha, there could be no doubt that it was true!

Bimbisara dismounted from his chariot and approached the Buddha on foot, with his Brahmins right behind him, scowling. They and their religion had never had a rival before, and they did not like to see these new beliefs growing so quickly.

King Bimbisara could not help noticing the change in his old acquaintance. Gautama's skin glowed, as if lit from within. His eyes saw clear through the king, right down to the innermost truth. His smile was blissful, free from all care.

*Yes, there is no doubt,* thought Bimbisara. He bowed low before the Buddha and said, "Teach me, I beg you, O Blessed One. From this day on, I am your follower—my Brahmins will also become your followers!"

At this, the Brahmins started to protest, but one look from their king made them keep silent. "My entire kingdom is at your disposal," Bimbisara went on. "Please stay here in my pleasure garden and make it your permanent home."

"I thank you, my friend," said the Buddha. "You are most generous, and I see that you seek earnestly to learn. Come, then, and sit by me."

From that day on, the Sangha grew by leaps and bounds. Citizens of Magadha joined the ranks of believers by the thousands. Rich citizens donated land, making the encampment large and comfortable. Shelters were erected so that the monks and students would stay dry through their rainy season retreat. Food was donated in abundance.

Soon, the fame of the Buddha reached Sakya itself. Word of his son's successes came to old Lord Shuddhodana and his court, within the walls of Kapilavastu Castle.

"Why has my son not come here to visit his homeland?" the lord asked his courtiers. "Is he angry with us? Why has he favored Magadha above his own home?" Shuddhodana sent a messenger to Rajagaha, inviting Siddhartha to come home.

But when he saw the messenger, the Buddha immediately began sharing the Great Law of the Dharma with him. Forgetting even to deliver his message, the messenger decided then and there to stay, and become part of the Sangha.

When Shuddhodana heard what had happened, he sent more messengers—but the same thing happened again and again! It was only on the tenth try, when he sent a childhood friend of Siddhartha's to deliver the message, that the Buddha accepted the invitation to return to Sakya, the land of his birth.

# CHAPTER TWELVE

# HOME AGAIN

By the time it arrived outside the walls of Kapilavastu, the Sangha numbered twenty thousand people. From the tower of his palace, Lord Shuddhodana could see the dust cloud that arose from the shuffling of so many feet along the road.

"Prepare the Banyan Monastery for them," he ordered. "And announce to one and all that my son Siddhartha, the prince of Sakya, has returned."

Soon the word was being passed around the palace and through all the streets of the capital. "Our prince has returned!" they told one another. "Our cousin, our friend, our country-man who has done so well in the world!" They immediately began calling him "Sakyamuni"—the Sage of Sakya.

The people of Kapilavastu were proud of their native son, but they had not yet even seen him, or heard his teaching. So they were surprised the next morning to find Siddhartha, along with his many disciples, begging for food in the main square of the city.

When he heard about this, Lord Shuddhodana was furious. Old man that he was, he marched down to the main square with his courtiers to see this spectacle for himself.

He barely recognized his son. It had been seven long years, and when he left, Siddhartha had been dressed in royal silks. Now, he wore the coarse orange robe of a monk and held a wooden begging bowl in his hands.

"Are you trying to shame me?" asked his father. "This is the city where you used to ride triumphant in your silks and cloth of gold. This whole country could have belonged to you! Even now, you could be feasting with me in my palace. Why then do you come here to the public square and beg for your food?"

"Pardon me, Father, for I did not mean to shame you," said the Buddha. "It is our custom to beg for food each day."

"It is not 'our custom'!" thundered Shuddhodana. "Our custom is to live like the nobles we are!"

"I meant the custom of sages," the Buddha explained patiently. "For I am now part of a long line of such holy men."

Lord Shuddhodana was still not happy. Again and again, he begged his son to come and dine at the palace. "Come and teach me, and all of my court," he said. At last, the Buddha agreed to come.

When he heard his son explain the Four Noble Truths and the Eightfold Path, Lord Shuddhodana finally understood once and for all that Siddhartha had become someone much more important than any king could ever be.

"Kings and kingdoms come and go," he told his courtiers, "but truly, the Great Law of the Dharma is eternal, and can be sought and understood by anyone in the world. My son, the prophecy of the sage Asita has indeed come true. Although I am old and cannot follow you on your travels, please count me among your disciples."

The Buddha embraced his father and welcomed him into his teaching. "And now," said Shuddhodana, "there are some others who wish very much to see you."

He gestured to another chamber, off to the side of the great banquet hall, where the Buddha's wife, Princess Yasodhara, waited to greet him after seven long years apart. There with her was their son, Rahula, now seven years old.

Yasodhara could see that the man who had been her husband had been utterly transformed and was now someone totally different. As sad as she had been when he left her side forever, she was happy now to see that he had found enlightenment and was beginning to share it with all humankind.

★  ★  ★  ★

Many Sakyans joined the Sangha during the Buddha's first visit home. Among them was Rahula, who decided to follow his father into the holy life. This distressed Lord Shuddhodana greatly, for he had hoped that Rahula would rule Sakya after he was gone.

Shuddhodana pleaded with his son. Finally, he convinced the Buddha to make a rule that from then on, no young person could join the Sangha without his parents' permission. Still, Rahula remained a monk, and Shuddhodana knew he would have to find a successor elsewhere.

Another convert to the Buddha's teaching was his younger cousin Ananda, who would soon become his master's closest aide. He would remain by the Buddha's side for the rest of his life.

His cousin and sometime rival Devadatta also joined the Sangha. All his life, Devadatta had been jealous of Siddhartha, who had bested him time and time again. Now that everyone was leaving town to follow the Buddha, he too, joined the crowd.

But in his heart, hidden away, he still nursed a deep hatred and jealousy of his cousin. When Devadatta joined the Sangha, the seeds of trouble were planted. They would soon grow into a dangerous, poisonous flower.

# CHAPTER THIRTEEN

# DEVADATTA'S REVENGE

In all, it is said that eighty thousand Sakyans joined the Sangha during the Buddha's first visit—one for each family in the land. The Buddha promised to return again, then led his growing horde of followers back to Vulture's Peak.

Only after they had returned did the Buddha learn that his foster mother, Japiti, had followed him. Now she approached him boldly. "When you were a baby, I raised you as my own," she said. "Now I ask you to accept me into the Sangha as a nun."

The Buddha was shocked. He had many women lay followers. But none had ever asked to become a nun, to give up her life and home and take up the life of a beggar. Now, his own stepmother was asking him!

He knew that if he allowed her to join the Sangha, many of his followers would not like it. The Brahmins especially were bound to be shocked and upset. He turned to his cousin Ananda and asked him what he thought it would be best to do.

"Blessed One," said Ananda, "if women were allowed to follow the Eightfold Path, do you believe they could reach enlightenment?"

"Certainly," the Buddha said.

"Well, then, surely it would be a good thing if women could be ordained into the Sangha as nuns—especially the woman who nursed you when you were a baby."

The Buddha agreed, and from then on, women were accepted into the order. Yasodhara herself soon became a follower. So did many others—and not just highborn women, either.

One day, Ananda was begging in town,

when he spied a young woman at a well, carrying a jug of water. "Sister," he called to her, "what is your name?"

"Prakriti, sir," she answered.

"Please, Prakriti, give me a drink, for I am thirsty."

The young woman shrank back from him. "Oh, no, sir," she replied. "I am an untouchable, and not worthy to give you drink."

"I am not talking about your caste, or your rank," said Ananda. "Please. I am thirsty. I am only asking for water."

So she gave him water to drink, and also fell in love with him. When he returned to the ashram, she followed him there, and with the aid of a love potion, tried to get him to love her back.

The potion did not work, for Ananda's devotion to the Sangha was too strong. Seeing that he would not give up his holy life to be with her, Prakriti gave up trying to win his heart. Instead, she began to listen avidly to the teachings of the Buddha. Soon, she, too, asked to become a nun.

When the Buddha granted her wish, the noble Brahmins of Savatthi, where the Sangha was staying at that time, objected. Not only was the Buddha accepting women into the order, now he was accepting untouchable women as well!

The Buddha had to convince the king of Savatthi that the caste system was unjust, and that lowborn people could act as nobly as those of high birth. In the end, the king, like nearly everyone the Buddha met, became convinced of the truth of the Middle Way.

Over the years, the Sangha continued to grow by leaps and bounds. Monasteries and ashrams sprang up all over northeastern India. They all looked to the Buddha for guidance, and he often traveled among them with his closest followers. He had become a very influential man, whose wisdom was respected by kings and commoners alike. One time, he even prevented a war.

Sakya and the neighboring kingdom of

Koliya were separated by the River Rohini. One year, in the dry season, there was not enough water to grow crops on both sides of the river. The Koliyans decided to divert the river so that they could get all its water for themselves. The Sakyans were outraged, and soon, two armies faced each other, ready to go to war.

Lord Shuddhodana had passed away by this time, but the ruler of Sakya was a member of Siddhartha's family. So was the king of Koliya—Siddhartha's mother, Maya, and his stepmother, Japiti, were both princesses of Koliya.

When the Buddha heard about this, he called the two rulers to his side and asked, "Tell me, how much is this spoonful of water worth?"

The kings laughed. "Why, very little!" they both said.

"And how much is the blood of your people worth?" the Buddha asked.

"Ha—a tremendous amount!" both rulers agreed.

"Then why spill precious blood over something that is so unimportant?" the Buddha reasoned. "In doing so, you may be cutting short the journey to enlightenment of many, many souls."

Putting an arm around each of their shoulders, he continued, "Let us live lives that are free of hatred, even if the rest of the world is full of hate."

The two rulers bowed their heads, seeing the great wisdom of the Buddha's argument. There would be no war between them, not then, or ever afterward.

Still, all was not peaceful everywhere else—not even within the Sangha. As the order grew larger, and the Buddha grew older, differences of opinion among his followers often erupted into conflict.

Some of the monks said their leader was growing too old, and his ideas needed to be updated. Others objected to the inclusion of women in the Sangha as nuns. Still others insisted on following the original Eightfold Path exactly, in all its details.

Devadatta had quietly made himself part of the Sangha, but in his heart, he was still jealous of his cousin. As much as everyone else loved the Buddha, Devadatta hated him. Now, seeing his moment, he hatched a plan.

One day, while the Buddha was off visiting his old friend King Bimbisara, Devadatta challenged his cousin's leadership of the Sangha, saying, "We monks following the Middle Way have been living too easy a life! What we need is a return to the hardships of the ascetics!"

A few monks agreed with him, while many others were shocked and dismayed. When news of this rebellion reached the Buddha, he sent word that Devadatta was to be kicked out of the Sangha at once.

From that day on, Devadatta began plotting, not just against the Sangha, but against his cousin's life. "Siddhartha has become so great, and has so many followers," he muttered to himself. "I am as smart and as wise as he is, and yet he has always bested me. Well, no longer!"

He went to see King Bimbisara's son, Ajatasattu, who had long wished to be king in his father's place. Devadatta knew this, and he knew his words would find fertile ground in the prince's heart.

"Your father gets older and older, yet he does not die," Devadatta whispered in his ear. "If you do not do something about it, you will never get to be king yourself!"

"What are you suggesting?" asked Ajatasattu.

"Your father and my cousin are often together," Devadatta said. "Let us strike hard, and get rid of them both at once!"

Ajatasattu agreed, and the two of them agreed to hire killers to do away with their two enemies. First, these assassins murdered King Bimbisara. Then they went to the bamboo grove, meaning to kill the Buddha as well.

But it so happened that when they arrived,

the Buddha was in the middle of one of his sutras, or sermons. Listening, the assassins were struck by his words. They dropped their knives, fell to their knees, and begged to be accepted into the Sangha.

Having succeeded in killing his father, Ajatasattu was now King of Magadha—but since he personally had nothing against the Buddha, Devadatta realized that he would now have to kill his cousin himself.

The next day, he climbed to the top of Vulture's Peak, overlooking the bamboo grove. There, he loosened a large boulder and sent it toppling downward.

The Buddha was sitting in the lotus position, teaching his disciples, when several of them pointed upward and shouted, "Watch out!"

The Buddha did not move. He simply closed his eyes and meditated. Just as it was about to crush him, the boulder hit the hillside, split in a thousand pieces, and missed the Buddha on either side. One sliver of the rock grazed his arm, but that was all. Everyone who was there said it was a miracle he had not been killed.

Devadatta was not through yet, however. Once more, he tried to kill his cousin. He went into town and found a man who tamed elephants. From this man, he bought an elephant that was well known as a killer of men.

The next week, when he knew that the Buddha and his closest disciples were coming into the city, Devadatta gave the elephant alcohol to make it drunk. Then he beat it with sticks until it was angry enough to kill anyone in its path. Finally, he opened the gate of the elephant's pen and watched as it rushed madly at the Buddha and his followers.

When they saw the elephant racing toward them, the Buddha's disciples all ran away screaming in fear—all except Ananda, who remained at his master's side as always.

The Buddha saw the elephant too—but unlike the others, he was not afraid. He saw that the poor animal was suffering, and he gazed at it lovingly, with great sympathy for its pain.

As angry and drunk as the elephant was, it could still sense the great love being sent its way by this man, who seemed to glow with radiant light. The great beast stopped its charge, walked slowly up to the Buddha, and kneeled at his feet, bowing its head low.

The Buddha stroked the animal gently on its huge head, and turned to Ananda, smiling. "You see, cousin, hatred cannot be defeated with more hatred, but only with love."

And so, the hatred of Devadatta was defeated by the great love of the Buddha.

# CHAPTER FOURTEEN

# THE END OF THE BEGINNING

The Buddha continued preaching and teaching for forty-five long years. Now, nearing the end of his life, he had become old and frail. His faithful aide, Ananda, was always by his side, making sure he did not fall or stumble.

One day, there was a commotion in the monastery, and a stretcher was brought in with a sick old man on it. To everyone's surprise, it was none other than Devadatta!

Everyone knew that Devadatta had tried to kill the Buddha more than once. He had gone away for many years since then, living in disgrace, but now, here he was—and deathly ill, by the look of him.

"I beg you," he gasped, reaching out for the Buddha's hand, "please forgive me and accept me back into the Sangha. I realize now that you were destined for greatness. If only I hadn't been so jealous of you, how much better off I would have been!"

"Do not lament, cousin," said the Buddha, taking his hand. "May my love for you heal your illness, and may you go forward to reach Nirvana yourself!"

Buddha ordered the monks to take care of Devadatta. They did not want to—not only because they did not like him, but also because Devadatta had an awful fever with horrible sores.

"He who tends the sick, tends me!" the Buddha scolded them, washing Devadatta himself until the others took over, shamefaced.

Soon, miraculously, Devadatta got well again. It is said that he became a devout follower of the Buddha from that time on, and went on to reach enlightenment before the end of his life.

The Buddha continued traveling throughout the lands of northern India, preaching sutras about the Noble Truths and the Eightfold Path. His followers numbered in the hundreds of thousands now, and new monasteries were springing up all the time.

But while his teachings were spreading, the Buddha knew that the time would soon come when the Sangha would have to continue on without him. He was greatly concerned about dying, not because he feared death—far from it, for with this death he would reach Nirvana—but because he did not want his teachings to be forgotten after he was gone.

In his eightieth year, while on winter retreat, the Buddha became ill. This illness was quite painful, although he never complained about it. Still, it was clear to him that his death was approaching. "I wish to return home one more time to Kapilavastu," he told Ananda. "I want to die in the city of my birth."

"No! Master, don't speak of dying!" Ananda

wailed. "You have guided us so perfectly in the direction of the truth—how will we continue without you?"

"My friend Ananda, don't cry and suffer on my account. Haven't I always told you that death is an essential part of life? And what use is it to fear death, which is nothing more than the fulfillment of our nature?

"Please do not forget what I have taught you. Do not say, 'My teacher is gone!' I have shared with you the Great Law of the Dharma— the Four Noble Truths and the Eightfold Path. Let these be your guide and teacher when I am gone. If you truly take these lessons to heart, you will not need me anymore. Now, please, let us get ready for our journey."

The trip began. The Buddha, too old to walk very far, was carried on a litter by his attendants.

One night, the Sangha was camped in a mango grove belonging to a man named Chunda. Chunda prepared a meal for the monks containing mushrooms, which the Buddha ate heartily and gratefully.

That night, the Buddha fell gravely ill. Whether something was wrong with those mushrooms or whether it was just his illness getting worse, no one will ever know.

Ananda and his other close companions grew very worried. But the Buddha insisted they continue on their way to Kapilavastu. He must have wanted very much to see his home one last time.

Soon they reached a place called Kusinara, on the banks of the River Hiranavati. There they stopped, because the Buddha was now so ill, he could clearly go no farther. "Ananda, lay me down there, in that grove of sala trees."

Ananda prepared a couch for his master between two of the trees, and laid the Buddha down upon it.

"Thank you, Ananda," he whispered. "This is where I will end my days on Earth."

He spent that entire day with the people of

the village, who came for advice or just for a blessing from the famous saint.

When they were gone for the night, Buddha asked Ananda to gather his closest disciples. He wanted to speak to them one last time.

"All of you," he began, "please remember what I have always taught you: that all suffering, discontent, and unhappiness is caused by desire and craving. Everything changes, so you must not become attached to anything. Do not seek light or refuge outside yourselves, either in false gods or in foolish cravings. Do not depend upon anyone else. Be your own light, your own refuge.

"All things that are born must die. Everything that grows must decay. Change is the way of nature. The true Buddha is not a human body—it is enlightenment itself. The human body must perish and dissolve—only the Great Law of the Dharma is eternal. Follow the Dharma and you will be true to me.

"My dear ones, in a moment, I shall pass into Nirvana. Please—devote yourselves to the

Great Law with all your heart. Work hard to find your own path to enlightenment."

With that, the Buddha turned onto his right side, laid his head in his right hand, and closed his eyes forever. One of the kindest men who ever lived—and surely, one of humanity's greatest teachers—passed into Nirvana, and into history.

# CHAPTER FIFTEEN

# BUDDHISM AFTER THE BUDDHA

Legend says that they took the Buddha's body into the castle at Kusinara. There they built a funeral pyre and tried to burn the body, as was the custom in India. But no one could light the pyre!

Many times they tried, but the wood refused to ignite. Finally, just when they had all given up, the entire pile of logs, with the body on top, caught fire in an instant and was consumed in a flame so hot and so brilliant that nothing was left but a few jugs' worth of ashes. These jugs were divided among the Buddha's closest disciples, to be taken to all parts of the world, where temples could be built around them.

As the Buddha had predicted, however, it was not his body that would live on. It was his teaching. And for a while, it looked as though that teaching would not long survive its master.

Right away, arguments began within the Sangha. Some monks wanted to change the rules right away. It was clear to Ananda and the rest of the Buddha's closest disciples that the survival of the Sangha, and of the Middle Way itself, was in danger.

Kassapa of Uruvela said, "We must create a full and true record of everything our master taught us, before it is too late!"

They all agreed to call a conference of the highest-ranking monks of the order. King Ajatasattu of Magadha was asked to host the conference at his palace, and agreed to do so.

At the conference, Ananda, Kassapa, Upali, and other top-ranking monks of the Sangha worked to remember every word of the Buddha's teaching, making sure they had every sutra memorized in exactly the same way, every idea of their master's correctly understood.

They also memorized the Great Law of the Dharma, and the rules of conduct for monks and nuns. Memorizing was necessary, remember, because writing had still not come to that part of the world.

The collected teachings of the Buddha were divided in three parts: the Vinaya (rules for the Sangha), the sutras (sermons of the Buddha), and the Abhidharma (comments on the teaching by members of the Sangha).

The conference lasted seven months. When it was over, and the members of the Sangha were ready to leave for the four corners of the world, they agreed that in one hundred years' time there would be another such conference. At this second conference, their successors would be able to check up on the state of things, and to make sure everyone still remembered everything the same way. (It was only at the *fourth* such conference, in the year A.D. 80, that the Buddha's teachings would finally be written down once and for all.)

By the time of the second conference, many things had changed. The kingdoms of northern India were all at war with one another. The Sangha, too, began to divide into arguing groups. Most of the arguments were over the rules for the Sangha, and how strict they should be.

At the third conference, 150 years later, the Sangha split into two schools: the Mahayana and the Theraveda. Theraveda was the stricter of the two schools. The Mahayana group had many branches, but all were in favor of changes in the original rules, arguing that these rules needed to be updated with the passing of so many years.

At that time, the great Emperor Asoka had managed to conquer and unite all of India. Over the years, he had fought many wars and was responsible for the deaths of thousands of people. Now, later in life, he regretted all the violence he had engaged in. He gave himself over to the teachings of the Buddha and ordered that all of India, and all the other lands he had conquered, should do the same. Under Asoka, Buddhism spread throughout the world. Even when his empire broke up, Buddhism remained strong in many lands.

Today, Theraveda Buddhism exists in Thailand, Myanmar, Sri Lanka, Cambodia, Laos, Vietnam, and other countries.

Mahayana Buddhism spread north of the Himalayas, and split into many branches. Tibetan Buddhism is one. Zen Buddhism is another. Japan, China, Tibet, Taiwan, and Korea all feature branches of Mahayana Buddhism.

Tibetan and Zen Buddhism, as well as Japan's Nichiren Buddhism, have found many followers in the West, including the United States. Westerners seem to like many things about Buddhism: It does not require belief in any god or gods. It is gentle, nonviolent, and antiwar. It believes in the equality and dignity of all living things. It encourages people to think independently, to transform themselves, and to seek and find their own way to true happiness.

The teachings of the Buddha have now been around for 2,500 years. In all that time, Buddhism has never shed blood in the Buddha's name. Nor has it tried to convert nonbelievers by force. Perhaps this is because Buddhism is not a "faith" so much as a way of living. Those who wish to follow it are always welcome, but it is always their decision.

Buddhism encourages us to get rid of our hatred, greed, selfishness, and fear. If we succeed, it tells us, we too, can become Buddhas. We too, can find the same perfect peace and understanding that Siddhartha Guatama found under the bodhi tree—and then, like him, go out and share it with the world.

# GLOSSARY

Abhidharma: comments on the teaching
of the Buddha by members of the Sangha,
codified after the Buddha's death.

Ajatasattu: Prince (and later king) of
Maghada, son of King Bimbisara, patron
of the Sangha after becoming king.

Alara Kalama: an early teacher, or guru,
of the future Buddha.

Ananda: Siddhartha's cousin, who later
became the Buddha's closest assistant, and
a leader of the Sangha. He helped codify his
master's teachings after the Buddha's death.

Anoma River: borders Sakya and the
Kingdom of Maghada.

Arjuna: a rival of Siddhartha's for Yasodhara's
hand in marriage. A great horseman.

Aryans: invaders from Central Asia who conquered northern India about 1500 B.C. and
brought their multigod religion with them.

Ascetic: a wandering monk who denies himself all the comforts of life, eating only one
meal a day, which he begs for, in hope of
achieving enlightenment.

Ashram: a school run by a yogi, also an
encampment of monks living with their
guru, or teacher.

Asita: the most famous yogi of his day. Lived
in a Himalayan cave, came to Kapilavastu
after a vision of Siddhartha's birth came to
him. Predicted Buddhahood for the baby.

Asoka: The Emperor who united all the lands
of northern India, centuries after the

Buddha's death. Asoka made Buddhism the official religion of his empire, helping to spread Buddhist beliefs all over the world.

Assaji: one of the five ascetics Siddhartha lived with before becoming the Buddha. An early member of the Sangha.

Bhallika: a traveling merchant who happened upon the Buddha just after he attained enlightenment, and became an early lay follower.

Banyan: a giant tree of northern India, also found in many other countries.

Benares: the greatest city of northeastern India in the Buddha's time. Now known as Varanasi.

Bhaddiya: one of the five ascetics Siddhartha lived with before becoming the Buddha. An early member of the Sangha.

Bhagava: a hermit and holy man whom Siddhartha met just after he left Sakya.

Bimbisara: King of Maghada, friend of the Buddha and patron of the Sangha. Father of Ajatasattu.

Boddhisatva: one who seeks Buddhahood.

Bodhi: a wild fig tree, also called a bo tree. Meditating all night under one of these, Siddhartha finally found perfect enlightenment and became the Buddha.

Brahmanism: the Aryans' religion. So complicated that only Brahmins could understand most of it.

Brahmins: members of the highest class, or caste, in Aryan/Indian society. They were priests, wise men, and spiritual advisers.

Buddha: a fully enlightened human being. The subject of this book, known as "the Buddha," was said to be the latest in a long line of such people. He alone, however, was able to share the path to enlightenment with the rest of the world.

Buddhism: the religion, or spiritual movement, founded by the Buddha's followers, based upon his teachings.

Channa: Siddhartha's faithful servant and groom, who was responsible for taking care of Kantaka.

Chunda: the owner of a mango grove on the way to Kapilavastu.

Devadatta: Siddhartha's cousin, and often, his rival. A great archer. Later, a member of the Sangha.

Dharma: the great law of Buddhist teaching, consisting of the Four Noble Truths and the Eightfold Path.

Gautama: the family name of the Buddha. The ruling Kshatriya clan of Sakya.

Gotami: a young woman who became an early lay follower of the Buddha.

Guru: a teacher, usually a sage, or yogi.

Himalaya: the tallest range of mountains in the world, they formed the northern borders of Sakya. In the Buddha's time, many holy men lived in caves there.

Hinduism: the majority religion in modern-day India, descended from the Brahmanic religion of the Aryans as well as other traditions.

Hiranavati: a river near Kapilavastu. Along its banks sat the village of Kusinara, where the Buddha passed from this life into Nirvana.

Indra: the ruling god of the Aryans. Also figures in modern Hinduism.

Japiti: a princess of Koliya; sister of Maya, second wife of Lord Shuddhodana, and aunt of Siddhartha. Raised him from the time he was a baby. First woman to join the Sangha as a nun.

Kantaka: Siddhartha's magnificent white horse.

**Kapilavastu:** the Buddha's home country, a republic ruled by the Gautama clan of Kshatriyas.

**Karma:** the law of cause and effect. Part of both Brahmanic and Buddhist beliefs, it says that everything we do or think has an effect, so it is best to act and think well so that good things may result.

**Kashmir:** a region bordering the Himalayas, famous for its wool and carpets. Today, it is divided and fought over between India and Pakistan.

**Kassapa:** the name of three different sages, all of whom became early members of the Sangha. One of these, Kassapa of Uruvela, or Mahakassapa, became a great leader of the Sangha after the Buddha's death, and helped codify his teachings.

**Koliya:** a kingdom bordering Sakya, separated from it by the Rohini River. Birthplace of princesses Maya and Japiti.

Kondanna: youngest of Lord Shuddhodana's wise men. A Brahmin, later a wandering ascetic and an early follower of the Buddha.

Kshatriyas: the warrior/noble class of Aryan/Indian societies, second in rank to Brahmins, often ruled kingdoms and republics.

Kusa: a form of soft grass, thought to be sacred, upon which Siddhartha sat on the night he became the Buddha.

Kusinara: a castle and village on the banks of the River Hiranavati, where the Buddha passed from this life into Nirvana.

Lay follower: one who does not give up his life to follow his guru, but believes in his teachings nevertheless.

Litter: a means for carrying noble passengers through the streets. Consisted of a tent with a board floor, resting on two long poles and carried by servants.

Lotus position: a cross-legged sitting posture, said to resemble a lotus flower. The right foot is placed on the left thigh and, if possible, the left foot goes onto the right thigh. The back is straight, but relaxed, and the hands are placed gently on the knees, palms up. Sitting in this position promotes healthful breathing and inner calm.

Lumbini Park: just outside Kapilavastu. Birthplace of Siddhartha.

Magadha: the kingdom bordering Sakya, separated from it by the Anoma River.

Mahanama: one of the five ascetics Siddhartha lived with before becoming the Buddha. An early member of the Sangha.

Mahayana: one of the two main branches of Buddhism, less strict and orthodox than Theraveda, the other branch. Forms of Mahayana Buddhism include Zen, Nichiren, Tibetan, and other variants.

Mahayana Buddhism is found today in Japan, China, Tibet, Taiwan, Korea, and Western countries as well.

Mara: the king of demons in Aryan/Indian religion. Tempted the future Buddha by appealing to his human weaknesses.

Maya: the princess of Koliya. Wife of Lord Shuddhodana, mother of Siddhartha.

Middle Way: part of the Buddha's teaching, meaning humans should neither indulge themselves too much nor deprive themselves too much.

Monasteries: sheltered places where monks live and study.

Nanda: a rival of Siddhartha's for Yasodhara's hand. A great swordsman.

Naranjana: a river cutting through the Uruvela forest.

Nirvana: the final liberation from the endless cycle of death and rebirth. Permanent enlightenment.

Pagoda tree: a tree whose leaves, when squeezed, yield a juice that stops bleeding and helps heal wounds.

Panchamas: outcastes, or untouchables. The lowest caste in Aryan/Indian society. They had to do the jobs no one else would do.

Persia: present-day Iran.

Pictograph: a picture meant to stand for a word. Pictographs are used by certain languages (e.g., Chinese, Japanese) instead of an alphabet where each letter stands for a sound.

Prakriti: an untouchable who fell in love with Ananda, and later became the first woman from the Panchama caste to join the Sangha as a nun.

Pyre: a pile of sticks or wood upon which a dead body is burned at a funeral.

Rahula: the son of Siddhartha and Yasodhara. The name means "a bond that holds you down." Later joined the Sangha.

Rajagaha: the capital city of the Kingdom of Magadha.

Rama: the god of death in the Aryan/Indian religion. Also figures in modern Hinduism.

Reincarnation: rebirth, the Aryan/Hindu belief that we are reborn again and again until we achieve enlightenment, or Nirvana, and step off the endless cycle of death and rebirth.

Rishi: a holy man, or sage.

Rishipatana: a deer park near Benares where the five ascetic companions went after splitting with Siddhartha Gautama.

Rohini: a river separating Sakya and Koliya.

Sakya: the Buddha's home country.

Sangha: the order of monks, and later nuns, founded by the Buddha.

Sanskrit: the language of the Aryan invaders, and the Brahmanic religion. In the conquered lands of northern India, only Brahmins spoke it.

Sari: a south-Asian garment consisting of several yards of lightweight cloth draped so that one end forms a skirt and the other a head or shoulder covering.

Savatthi: a kingdom of northeast India whose king became a devotee of Buddhism.

Serendib: modern-day Sri Lanka, an island nation south of India famous for its spices.

Shuddhodana: the first lord of Sakya, father of the Buddha. A Kshatriya noble of the Gautama clan.

Siddhartha: the first name of the future

Buddha. It means "He who has achieved his goal."

Sudras: the second-lowest caste, or class, in Aryan/Hindu societies. Little better than slaves, they did most of the manual labor and unappealing jobs.

Sujata: a young woman of the Uruvela forest who saved the future Buddha's life by giving him milk to drink when he was dying of hunger and thirst.

Sunita: an untouchable; a garbage-picker who became an early member of the Sangha.

Suprabuddha: the king of a land bordering Sakya; father of Yasodhara.

Sutras: the sermons of the Buddha, codified after his death by members of the Sangha.

Tapussu: a traveling merchant who happened upon the Buddha just after he attained enlightenment, and became an early lay follower.

Theraveda: one of the two main branches of Buddhism, the stricter and more orthodox of the two. (Mahayana is the other.) Theraveda is practiced today in Thailand, Myanmar, Sri Lanka, Cambodia, Laos, Vietnam, and other countries.

Uddaka Ramaputta: an early teacher, or guru, of the future Buddha.

Upali: a top-ranking monk of the Sangha, who helped codify Buddhist practice and belief after the Buddha's death.

Uruvela: a forest in the Kingdom of Magadha where many gurus lived, some with large ashrams.

Vaisyas: the third-highest caste in Aryan/Indian societies. They were the merchants, shopkeepers, and skilled tradesmen.

Vappa: one of the five ascetics Siddhartha lived with before becoming the Buddha. An early member of the Sangha.

Vinaya: rules for the Sangha, codified after the Buddha's death.

Vulture's Peak: a place outside Rajagaha where the Sangha encamped.

Yasodhara: princess; the daughter of King Suprabuddha, wife of Siddhartha, she later joined the Sangha.

Yogi (also called "yogin"): a sage widely acknowledged for his holiness. Many had their own ashrams, or schools.

# FOR MORE
# INFORMATION

Want to learn more about the life of Buddha, or about Buddhism? Try these books and websites:

## BOOKS

Armstrong, Karen. *Buddha*. New York: Penguin/Putnam, 2001.

Hesse, Hermann. *Siddhartha*. New York: Bantam Classics, 1981.

Hulskramer, George, illustrated by Bijay Raj

Shakya and Raju Babu Shakya. *The Life of Buddha: From Prince Siddhartha to Buddha*. Amsterdam, The Netherlands: Binkey Kok Publishing, 1995.

Ikeda, Daisaku. *The Living Buddha: An Interpretive Biography*. New York, Tokyo: Weatherill Books, 1976.

Kornfield, Jack, ed. *Teachings of the Buddha*. New York: Barnes & Noble, 1999.

Landaw, Jonathan, illustrated by Janet Brooke. *Prince Siddhartha: The Story of Buddha*. Somerville, MA: Wisdom Publications, 2003.

Lee, Jeanne M. *I Once Was a Monkey: Stories Buddha Told*. New York: Farrar, Straus and Giroux, 1999.

Nelson, Walter Henry. *Buddha: His Life and His Teaching*. London: Luzak Oriental Publishing, 1996. New York: Penguin/Putnam, 2000.

Nhat Hanh, Thich. *A Pebble for Your Pocket.* Berkeley: Plum Blossom Books, 2001.

Saddhatissa, Hammalawa. *Before He Was Buddha: The Life of Siddhartha.* Berkeley: Seastone/Ulysses Press, 1998.

## WEBSITES

General information on Buddhism:

www.beliefnet.com (click on Buddhism)

www.buddhanet.net

www.lucidate.com

Buddhism in America:

www.dharmaforkids.com (Mahayana Buddhism)

www.e-sangha.com (T-shirts, statues, chat rooms, etc.)

www.gakkaionline.net/kids (SGI's kids site)

www.hsuyun.org (Zen Buddhism)

www.sgi-usa.org (Nichiren Buddhism lay group)